Cuba and the New Caribbean Economic Order

Volume XV, Number 2

Significant Issues Series

Cuba and the New Caribbean Economic Order

by Ernest H. Preeg

with Jonathan D. Levine

The Center for Strategic
and International Studies
Washington, D.C.

Library of Congress Cataloging-in-Publication Data

Preeg, Ernest H.
    Cuba and the new Caribbean economic order / by Ernest H. Preeg, with
Jonathan D. Levine.
            p. cm. — (Significant issues series, ISSN 0736-7136 ; v. 15, no. 2)
    Includes bibliographical references.
    ISBN 0-89206-209-6
    1. Cuba—Economic conditions—1959 - 2. Cuba—Foreign economic rela-
tions. 3. Caribbean Area—Economic conditions—1945 - 4. Caribbean Area—
Foreign economic relations. I. Levine, Jonathan D. II. Title. III. Series.
HC152.5.P7 1993
337.72910729—dc20   93-2780
                                                                         CIP

Cultivo una rosa blanca,
En julio como en enero,
Para el amigo sincero
Que me da su mano franca.

Y para el cruel que me arranca
El corazón con que vivo,
Cardo ni oruga cultivo:
Cultivo la rosa blanca.

♦

I cultivate a white rose,
In July as in January,
For the sincere friend
Who gives me his open hand.

And for the cruel person who tears out
The heart with which I live,
Neither thistle nor wild rocket do I cultivate:
I cultivate the white rose.

José Martí
(1853 · 1895)

Contents

About the Authors   viii

Preface   ix

Executive Summary   xii

1. **The New Caribbean Economic Order**   **1**
   Three Growth Sectors   3
   The Three-Country Composite   9

2. **A Quantum Economic Setback for Castro**   **14**

3. **The Castro Reform Program**   **23**
   The Zero Option   23
   The U.S. Embargo Dimension   31

4. **Cuba Restructured: The Political Assumption**   **36**
   Lessons Learned from Eastern Europe   37
   Invidious Comparison with the Former Soviet Union   40

5. **The Cuba Restructured Plus Five Projection**   **45**
   The Components of Foreign Exchange Receipts   48
   The Macroeconomic Outlook   58
   The NAFTA Option   61

6. **The Impact on Others in the Region**   **65**
   Short-term Shifts in Trade and Investment   69
   Longer-term Growth and Restructuring   71
   What Next after NAFTA?   73

7. **The U.S. Policy Response**   **76**
   A Proactive Strategy   78
   Reconciliation: The Pervading Concept   83

Appendix:
   An Economic Assistance Strategy for Cuba   85

Notes   90

About the Authors

Ernest H. Preeg holds the William M. Scholl Chair in International Business at the Center for Strategic and International Studies (CSIS). As a foreign service officer, he held the positions of deputy assistant secretary of state for international finance and development (1976 – 1977), ambassador to Haiti (1981 – 1983), and chief economist and deputy assistant administrator of the U.S. Agency for International Development (1986 – 1988). His published works include *Haiti and the CBI: A Time of Change and Opportunity* (University of Miami, 1984) and *Neither Fish nor Fowl: U.S. Economic Aid to the Philippines for Noneconomic Objectives* (CSIS, 1991). He holds a Ph.D. in economics from the New School for Social Research.

Jonathan D. Levine is a research analyst for the William M. Scholl Chair in International Business at CSIS. A graduate of the University of Massachusetts at Amherst, he has worked extensively on international trade and Latin American issues.

Preface

The genesis of this study, in the fall of 1991, was my observation that two fundamental changes in the Cuba/Caribbean regional relationship were not being fully recognized, even by Cuba experts. The first was the enormity of the adverse impact on the Communist regime in Havana from the abrupt cutoff of Soviet aid and the collapse of the Soviet Union. The second change was a basic restructuring of the North American/Caribbean regional economic relationship during the 1980s that would offer highly favorable circumstances for a reintegration of a market-oriented Cuba into the region. The "objective conditions," to use the now-benign Marxist terminology, had changed fundamentally, while policy discussion of the U.S.-Cuba relationship continued in much the same terms as before.

The subsequent economic analysis presented here bears out this initial observation in even starker terms than I had anticipated. Not only is Cuba destined to become deeply integrated again with its regional neighbors, and most particularly with the United States, but an early restructuring to a market-oriented economy can produce a very quick and robust recovery from its present crisis situation. The most important conclusion of this study is that Fidel Castro is simply wrong when he tells the Cuban people that such a restructuring will cause the kind of economic collapse and chaos that is currently happening in Russia. As explained in detail in chapters 4 and 5, there are parallels with and lessons to be learned from the transition under way in the former Soviet bloc, but the differences between Russia and Cuba are far more important and are uniformly to Cuba's great comparative advantage.

The policy implications of this central analytic conclusion are complex and controversial, as has been evident during the considerable discussion of this study in draft form. Many Cuba experts do not believe the Cuban people would support a basic restructuring to a market economy even if they had the democratic opportunity to do so. Others predict an extended period of instability and violence when the inevitable political change occurs, which would preclude a successful economic recovery as projected here.

Perhaps these discouraging views carry the highest probability for the future course of Cuba, although it is worth noting that relatively peaceful democratization and radical economic reforms have taken place in most of Eastern Europe and the former Soviet Union, notwithstanding earlier expert opinion to the contrary. In any event, the "Cuba Restructured Plus Five" scenario contained in chapters 4 and 5 is not a prediction of the most likely outcome from this vantage point in time but, rather, a highly feasible projection, given the stated political and economic assumptions. The likelihood of this five-year projection being realized will depend on a number of factors. A better understanding within Cuba of this alternative to the current crisis would help. So, too, in my judgment, would the suggested U.S. policy response contained in chapter 7.

This project has benefited from a wide range of discussion and debate. An advisory committee of about 80 participants met in May, October, and December 1992. Committee membership was drawn from executive branch officials, congressional staffers, Cuba experts, and, most heavily, private-sector representatives from U.S., European, Canadian, and Japanese firms with actual or potential interests in Cuba. I had the opportunity to travel to Mexico, Venezuela, the Dominican Republic, Jamaica, and Trinidad (for a regional conference), where I conducted close to 70 interviews with private-sector leaders, government officials, and U.S. embassy officers, most of whom have had considerable exposure to Cuba. In December 1992, the analytic conclusions of the study were presented at the annual Caribbean/Latin America Action conference in Miami to an audience of more than 500, including nine expert commentators representing a wide range of viewpoint and background. To all of the above, I express my thanks for their most helpful comments, which greatly influenced and improved the final study presented here.

I was unable, however, to visit Cuba, despite repeated requests over a six-month period to the Cuba Interests Section in Washington. The Cuban response was negative, indicative of the closed society that currently prevails. I hope that in the critical period ahead a more open and forward-looking dialogue can be established between our two countries, as recommended in chapter 7.

I wish to express special gratitude to my colleague Jonathan Levine, who undertook most of the data gathering and analysis while also counseling me on all aspects of the study. Georges Fauriol, director of the Americas Program at CSIS, provided me with a broad political perspective, drawing on earlier Cuba studies at the Center. Additional valued assistance came from Brian Coyne, Greta Lovenheim, and Andrew Hamilton, who served, successively, as CSIS interns working on this project, and from Constance Kaczka for secretarial support throughout. Lastly, words cannot express my appreciation for my closest Cuba adviser from whom, among other things, I first heard "Cultivo una rosa blanca." She is my wife, Sally, although in her native Camagüey she was known as Salucha.

E. H. P.

Executive Summary

Since the early 1980s, the Caribbean regional economy has been undergoing fundamental change toward far deeper integration and, in particular, a more predominant dependency of the smaller countries in the region on the North American market. The composition of trade and investment has been shifting away from traditional agricultural commodities and toward other cash crop agriculture, tourism, assembly industry, and the service sector in general. Although this change is private-sector-driven, it has also received strong reinforcement from government initiatives: the U.S. Caribbean Basin Initiative (CBI), market-oriented economic reforms throughout the region, and the North American Free Trade Agreement (NAFTA), as a first step toward hemispheric free trade. The momentum is all toward further and deeper integration of the North American/Caribbean regional economy.

In this context, Cuba becomes an ever more glaring anomaly. In the 1950s, the Cuban economy was a leading hub of activity at the center of the regional economy. Now it is isolated, unconnected, and in decline. The abrupt end of Soviet economic support precipitated an unprecedented economic crisis that is causing a deterioration—or *desmoronamiento*—of the physical and human infrastructure of the country. The Castro government has implemented some reforms to reorient trade and investment away from its former 85 percent dependence on the Soviet bloc, but the most important and natural market—the United States—remains closed, while the response elsewhere in the hemisphere has been small.

Resolving the economic crisis in Cuba is urgent so as to minimize the longer-term consequences of the deterioration currently under way. But how is this possible, at what cost, and in what time frame? The obvious preferred route would be reintegration of Cuba into the regional economy, including the United States. But does the Castro government have an alternative?

This study addresses these questions, through quantitative economic projections to the extent feasible. The two limiting cases are, first, the modest reform program currently being implemented by the Castro government while the U.S. embargo remains in place and, second, a basic restructuring of Cuba to a market economy with a lifting of the U.S. embargo. The analysis is not limited to Cuba but extends to other countries in the Caribbean region, some of whose situations will be altered significantly, in some respects adversely, from a basic restructuring of the Cuban economy.

Such economic projections cannot be separated, however, from political implications and consequences. In any event, political assumptions need to be made as a basis for projecting an economic outcome. More important, a better understanding of the economic options facing Cuba should influence political judgment by all parties concerned. Indeed, with the end of cold war ideological confrontation, the economic costs and benefits of political decisions should carry greater weight.

The economic analysis developed here thus leads to policy issues of a political as well as economic character, and recommendations for U.S. policy are offered at the conclusion. The point of departure is that the severity of the economic crisis within Cuba and the greatly changed circumstances elsewhere in the region and in the world warrant a fresh and forward-looking policy assessment by the new administration in Washington. It would be encouraging to know that a similar reassessment was under way in Havana.

The principal analytic conclusions of the study are as follows:

1.   During the 1980s, Caribbean Basin economies became more dependent on the North American market while shifting the structure of their exports. Traditional agricultural commodity exports were flat or down, while foreign exchange earnings from nontraditional agriculture, assembly industry, and tourism rose sharply. By the decade's end, Caribbean island economies received $9 billion of tourism receipts compared with non-Cuban coffee and sugar exports of $796 million and $332 million, respectively. Assembly industry exports, 90 percent of which went to the United States, were another $2 billion.

2.   A "three-country composite"—Costa Rica, the Dominican Republic, and Jamaica, which together are about the same size as Cuba—demonstrates the contrast between this new Caribbean economic order and Cuba. In 1989, the last year of full Soviet eco-

nomic support for Cuba, the three countries had aggregate foreign exchange receipts of $8.7 billion, 60 percent of which came from manufactured exports, tourism, economic aid, and remittances, while only 2 percent was from sugar. Cuban aggregate foreign exchange receipts of $5.8 billion, in contrast, were still 67 percent dependent on sugar.

3.   The abrupt cutoff of Soviet aid has had a devastating impact on the Cuban economy. From 1989 to 1992, the overall economy declined an estimated 45 percent, while imports were cut by 73 percent, from $8.1 billion to $2.2 billion. Imports of foodstuffs were down by 41 percent, petroleum by two-thirds, and machinery and equipment by an extraordinary 86 percent. The last figure is causing the most serious consequences because it means that new investment projects and maintenance of economic infrastructure have ground to a halt, resulting in a cumulative deterioration of the industrial base of the economy.

4.   The current, limited reform program of the Castro government, which aims to attract foreign investment while the U.S. embargo remains in effect, will not achieve significant improvement, and the cumulative deterioration of the economy will continue. Foreign exchange receipts of $2.7 billion in 1992 are projected to 1995 in a range of $2.3 to $2.9 billion. Further decline in sugar exports will more than offset anticipated increases in tourist revenues. The projected change, in any event, is insignificant compared with the $6 billion drop in imports since 1989.

5.   A comprehensive five-year projection for a Cuba restructured fundamentally to a market-oriented economy, in conjunction with a lifting of the U.S. embargo, produces an early and dramatic recovery in the Cuban economy, with foreign exchange receipts doubling in two years from the 1992 level of $2.7 billion and rising to a projected $9.5 billion in year five.

6.   This five-year projection is based on the political assumption of a relatively nonviolent democratic and market-oriented transition in Cuba, although the political process would be confused and tense after three decades of Communist rule. There are parallels with and lessons to be learned from recent transition experiences in the former Soviet bloc, including the need to place early priority on developing a financial services sector and enabling new small and medium-sized private businesses to flourish.

7.   Even more important, however, are the differences between conditions in Cuba and Russia, which greatly favor Cuban prospects for a market-oriented economic recovery. Russia has many more industrial "dinosaurs," armed forces that are less employable in civilian life and more deep-seated environmental degradation. Most important, Cuba is situated at the center of the Caribbean regional economy, with wide-ranging export opportunities.

8.   The five-year projection for a restructured Cuba has two phases. During the first two years, the increase in foreign exchange receipts would come from tourism, remittances from expatriate Cubans, foreign aid, and trade credits. In the later years, growth would shift predominantly to private-sector-driven investment, exports, and more broadly based job creation in the economy.

9.   A market-oriented Cuba reintegrated into the Caribbean economy will have substantial impact on others in the region, primarily the island economies of the Dominican Republic, Jamaica, and the smaller members of the Caribbean Community and Common Market (CARICOM). There will be both "trade-creating" and "trade-diverting" effects, that is, Cuban growth in trade and investment will either add to or displace levels elsewhere in the region. Trade-creating effects are more likely for tourism, trade-diverting effects for assembly industry, with nontraditional agricultural exports somewhere in between.

10.   The accession of Cuba to NAFTA during the projected five-year period would bring even greater opportunities for strong economic recovery in two ways. It would increase Cuban access to the U.S. market for such sectors as textiles, auto parts, and fruits and vegetables, but not likely for sugar. It would also improve the investment climate in Cuba by broadening market-oriented reforms and making them irreversible.

The recommendations for U.S. policy derived from this assessment are as follows:

The central U.S. policy objective should remain the earliest possible transition of Cuba to democracy and market-oriented economic recovery. The policy response to the very changed circumstances in Cuba and in the Caribbean region, however, should be more proactive than in recent years, combining positive incentives to reform with disincentives to continued abuse of basic human rights and nondemocratic Communist rule. The three basic elements of the response should be a broadened dialogue, a more proactive bilateral agenda, and a concerted multilateral diplomacy.

- A *broadened and more open dialogue* should include various sectors of leadership and expertise in both countries. In political terms, the United States should explain its support for democratization as it relates to Cuban sovereignty. In economic terms, the options facing Cuba at this crisis stage should be analyzed with the participation of economists who currently deal with Eastern Europe and U.S. business leaders who have actual or potential interests in the Caribbean region.
- A *more proactive bilateral agenda* should be tailored to circumstances as they evolve in Cuba and could involve targeted incentives, such as trade in humanitarian-related goods. A full lifting of the embargo would not be advisable, however, absent a clear commitment by Cuba to an irrevocable course of democratization and economic reform.
- A *concerted multilateral diplomacy*, in addition to action in the United Nations (UN) Human Rights Commission, should exert pressures for reform within Cuba by the United States together with its hemispheric neighbors and Cuba's industrialized trading partners. A less confrontational attitude by the United States should enable a more concerted approach even while the embargo is still in effect.

Finally, a broad theme of reconciliation, both among Cubans and between Cuba and the United States, should pervade this more proactive policy response. Communist political rule and state-controlled national economies are spent concepts of the past. The economic realities of the new Caribbean economic order offer strong mutual interests and opportunities for the future.

1
The New Caribbean
Economic Order

The 1980s are frequently referred to as the "lost decade" for development, a period of crushing external debt, hyperinflation, and economic stagnation. The Caribbean regional economy suffered these afflictions, but at the same time, and largely in response to them, experienced a basic transformation that has opened a far more hopeful economic prospect for the decade ahead. North America, including Mexico, Central America, the Caribbean island economies—except Cuba—and, to a lesser extent, Venezuela and Colombia, have become a more deeply integrated regional economy, dedicated to export-led growth, and the process continues.[1]

The dilemma created by the earlier development strategy of high protection for domestic industry in tandem with reliance on exports of traditional agricultural commodities and industrial raw materials is now well known. The protected domestic industry still required a large share of imported components, while the market for traditional commodity exports expanded slowly if at all. Population growth in rural areas spilled into the cities, where new industrial jobs increased the import bill. A growing trade deficit could be financed for a while through borrowing abroad, but then came the financial crisis and economic impasse—the predicament of most Caribbean Basin countries in the early 1980s.

The U.S. Caribbean Basin Initiative (CBI) of 1982, which increased economic aid and expanded free entry to the U.S. market for Central American and Caribbean countries, was based, above all, on a revised development strategy of open trade, increased international investment, and a more interdependent regional economy. The challenge from the point of view of the smaller Caribbean economies was summed up by Prime Minister Edward Seaga of Jamaica:

Table 1.1
U.S. Imports of Agricultural Commodities from Caribbean Basin Countries[a]
(in millions of U.S. dollars)

Country	Traditional Commodities[b]			Other Agriculture		
	1980	1985	1990	1980	1985	1990
Colombia	937	588	564	88	150	225
Costa Rica	207	222	248	75	72	152
Dominican Republic	409	321	205	46	80	98
El Salvador	286	239	95	8	10	12
Guatemala	328	271	368	45	61	127
Honduras	239	226	204	83	39	50
Jamaica	28	14	12	6	20	21
Mexico	336	380	412	723	910	2,198
Venezuela	16	30	7	2	6	16
All others	304	204	88	118	47	49
Total for all Caribbean Basin countries	**3,090**	**2,495**	**2,203**	**1,194**	**1,395**	**2,948**

Source: U.S. Department of Agriculture, Economic Research Service, Commodity Economics Division, *Foreign Agricultural Trade of the United States (FATUS)* (Washington, D.C., 1980, 1985, 1990).
[a] Mexico, Central America, Colombia, Venezuela, and the Caribbean island economies except Cuba.
[b] Coffee, cocoa, sugar, and bananas (including products).

Gearing our economies to take serious advantage of the new export opportunities requires a fundamental psychological adjustment to accompany the necessary structural changes that must occur when we move, for example, from import substitution to export directed production.[2]

This psychological adjustment, as well as the economic restructuring, proved more daunting than initially anticipated. By mid-decade, however, a number of countries in the region were shifting to a more export-oriented economy, which also meant a growing dependency on the huge and proximate North American market. The definitive change for the region was the radical reform program in Mexico, begun in 1986 and culminating with the North American Free Trade Agreement (NAFTA) of 1992. The Mexican example of private-sector-driven open trade and investment was increasingly emulated throughout the region by the decade's end, with profound results.

Three Growth Sectors

The most important and graphic results can be observed in three sectors: agriculture, assembly industry, and tourism.

Agriculture

The shift in exports from traditional commodities—sugar, bananas, coffee, and cocoa—to other agricultural products, including citrus fruit, tomatoes, pineapples, mangoes, melons, and cut flowers—is shown in table 1.1. U.S. imports of the traditional commodities from the Caribbean Basin declined steadily from $3.1 billion in 1980 to $2.2 billion in 1990. The decline was most pronounced for sugar, with U.S. imports dropping by more than half, from $753 million in 1980 to $326 million in 1990.[3] U.S. imports of other, "nontraditional" agricultural products, in contrast, rose from $1.2 billion in 1980 to $1.4 billion in 1985 and then even more sharply to $2.9 billion in 1990. Mexico was most prominent in expanding other agricultural exports, reflecting both the size of the Mexican economy and the early effects of the Mexican trade liberalization program, but other smaller Caribbean countries also registered substantial gains during the second half of the decade.

Table 1.2
OECD and U.S. Imports of Manufactures from Caribbean Basin Countries[a]
(in millions of U.S. dollars)

Country	All OECD Imports			U.S. Imports			U.S. Share of Total (percent)
	1980	1985	1990	1980	1985	1990	1990
Mexico	4,103	9,118	22,430	1,737	8,181	19,602	87.4%
All Others	2,071	3,211	7,143	959	2,372	4,717	66.0
Columbia	343	365	914	164	245	525	57.4
Costa Rica	70	176	607	60	169	575	94.7
Dominican Republic	295	505	1,437	230	434	1,296	90.2
Guatemala	21	35	255	15	30	245	96.1
Haiti	231	378	364	213	361	329	90.4
Jamaica	23	88	322	19	82	292	90.7
Panama	268	301	867	11	89	89	10.3
Venezuela	195	352	894	73	270	512	57.3
Others	625	1,011	1,483	174	692	854	57.6
Total for all Caribbean Basin countries	6,174	12,329	29,573	2,696	10,553	24,319	82.2%

Source: OECD Import-Export trade data microfiche.
[a] Mexico, Central America, Colombia, Venezuela, and the Caribbean island economies except Cuba.

Up-to-date statistics on global agricultural exports of Caribbean countries are not readily available, especially for the Other Agriculture category. Sluggish markets for basic commodities during the 1980s, however, are confirmed at the global level. For sugar, total Caribbean Basin exports, excluding Cuba, declined from $969 million in 1989 to $809 million in 1990. For coffee, export revenues were down over the same period from $4.8 billion to $3.0 billion.[4]

Assembly Industry

Caribbean Basin exports of manufactures, largely derived from assembly industry, also expanded rapidly during the 1980s, gathering momentum in the second half of the decade. Such labor-intensive industry can be established quickly through the construction of industrial parks and accompanying transportation and communications infrastructure. Production and exports can be under way within a year of ground breaking. The critical factor is a government policy framework that provides the incentives for export-oriented industry. Exchange rates, port and utility costs, labor practices, and tax rates are among the determining factors. The costs and administrative delays of a highly protectionist trading system can be circumvented through the creation of free trade zones that effectively operate outside the national customs territory.

The creation of an overall positive investment climate for assembly industry in the Caribbean region was a learning process during the 1980s, with early results in Mexico and Haiti later emulated elsewhere, as shown in table 1.2. The figures are for Organization for Economic Cooperation and Development (OECD) imports of manufactures from the Caribbean Basin countries, because export statistics for Caribbean countries are not generally available, often lag by a number of years, and, in some instances, such as for Mexico and the Dominican Republic, exclude exports from free trade zones. Imports by the industrialized OECD countries nevertheless represent the overwhelming majority of total manufactured exports by these countries.

Total manufactured imports by OECD countries from Caribbean Basin countries doubled from $6.2 billion in 1980 to $12.3 billion in 1985 and then more than doubled again to $29.6

Table 1.3
Growth in Caribbean Tourism

Year	Number of hotel rooms (thousands)	Hotel guests (millions)	Cruise arrivals (millions)	Total tourist expenditures ($ U.S. billions)
1985	86.9	7.8	4.0	5.0
1986	90.5	8.4	5.1	5.7
1987	95.7	9.6	5.7	6.7
1988	101.6	10.2	6.3	7.3
1989	107.2	10.9	6.8	8.0
1990	112.3	11.5	7.5	8.7
Average annual growth	5.3%	8.1%	13.6%	11.8%

Source: World Tourism Organization, *Yearbook of Tourism Statistics*, vols. 1 and 2 (Madrid, Spain, 1990-1992).

billion in 1990. The largest supplier by far was Mexico, with exports up from $4.1 billion to $22.4 billion during the course of the decade. But other Caribbean Basin exporters also showed strong gains, especially in the second half of the decade, more than doubling exports from $3.2 billion in 1985 to $7.1 billion in 1990. The United States was the largest single market, and the U.S. market share increased sharply from 44 percent in 1980 to 82 percent in 1990. The Caribbean island economies, including the Dominican Republic, Haiti, and Jamaica, all showed a greater than 90 percent U.S. market share by the end of the decade, which is relevant to Cuban export potential once the embargo is lifted.

Tourism

The Caribbean island economies in particular have benefited since the mid-1980s from rapid growth in the tourism sector, much more rapid than the growth in tourism globally. Natural endowments of weather and beaches, aggressive investment and marketing programs by hotel and cruise ship companies, and the general trend toward more service-oriented consumption spending have contributed to this remarkable expansion.

A full account of revenues and employment in the Caribbean tourism sector is not possible. Existing data are more complete for hotel than for cruise ship visitors and are sketchy for other support services dependent on tourism. Both seasonal and business cycle factors can have substantial impact on hotel occupancy rates. The year 1991 was disappointing, not only because of the recession in the United States but also because of the Persian Gulf War, which inhibited vacation air travel.

Some basic indicators presented in table 1.3, however, give a rough idea of growth for Caribbean island tourism. From 1985 to 1990, the number of hotel guests increased by 8 percent per year, while cruise passenger arrivals increased at a much faster rate, about 14 percent per year. Total expenditures by hotel guests and cruise passengers are estimated to have grown almost 12 percent per year, reaching a level of $8.7 billion in 1990. Five destinations—the Bahamas, the Dominican Republic, Jamaica, Puerto Rico, and the U.S. Virgin Islands— accounted for close to half of total expenditures.

U.S. visitors constituted the largest share of Caribbean

tourism, but the level varies considerably within the region. For the larger islands closer to the United States, including the five noted above that are most relevant to future prospects for Cuba, the U.S. share of tourism is in the 60 percent to 80 percent range, while for the smaller, more distant islands the U.S. share is lower.[5] Because U.S. visitors tend to stay for a shorter time than Europeans and others coming from further away, however, the U.S. share of total expenditures is somewhat lower.

These three high-growth sectors—nontraditional agriculture, assembly industry, and tourism—illustrate both the magnitudes and the rate of change within the regional Caribbean economy. Traditional agricultural commodity exports to the U.S. market have been overtaken by other farm products. Manufactured exports, mostly assembly industry, were more than double total agricultural exports to the United States by 1990. As for Caribbean island economies, a $9 billion tourism industry in 1990 compares with non-Cuban coffee exports of $796 million, sugar exports of $332 million, and banana exports of $329 million.

This is not a complete assessment of the transformation under way within the regional economy. Other service sector industries, including transportation, construction, financial services, and wide-ranging information technology activities, are all expanding within the region, but comprehensive data are not available. The overall picture is nevertheless clear. The labor force throughout the region is rapidly moving away from traditional agricultural commodities and protected industry toward a wide range of more export-competitive manufacturing and service industries that are generating high economic growth and increased employment. This process, by definition, is creating an increasingly open and more deeply interdependent regional economy, with the smaller countries particularly dependent on the North American market, predominantly the United States. A political consequence of this economic transformation is that the smaller economies are far more constrained in the exercise of their economic sovereignty, which would become more formalized if they were to join NAFTA. The implications of all of the above for Cuba, as described in later chapters, are enormous.

The Three-Country Composite

To obtain a more precise idea of the likely trade and investment relationships that could evolve for a reintegrated Cuba, a more detailed analysis was made of three selected countries in the region: Costa Rica, the Dominican Republic, and Jamaica. This three-country composite constitutes a cross section of the smaller-sized regional economies and, as shown in table 1.4, together the three are of similar size to Cuba. The population of the three in 1990 was somewhat larger than that of Cuba—13.0 million versus 10.7 million. The total arable land was about a third smaller—2.2 versus 3.3 million square kilometers. There are also, however, more striking contrasts. The share of arable land devoted to sugar is 41 percent in Cuba compared with only 13 percent in the three-country composite. The acreage devoted to sugar in Cuba is therefore more than five times that in the three-country composite (1,350 versus 285 thousand square kilometers). Per capita energy consumption in Cuba was also 77 percent higher than in the three other countries and almost three times as high as that of the Dominican Republic. This reflects the highly energy-intensive sugar and nickel industries in Cuba and the general inefficiency of energy consumption that prevails in Cuba in the absence of market-oriented prices. The number of telephones per capita in Cuba is only one-third to one-half the levels in the three other countries, indicating a much weaker telecommunications capability.

Even more important and relevant contrasts for the future development of Cuba are those concerning exports and other sources of foreign exchange receipts. Total foreign exchange receipts constitute the central constraint on economic growth and development for the relatively small Caribbean Basin economies. A comparison of the three-country composite and Cuba is presented in table 1.5 for five principal categories of foreign exchange receipts, which together constitute close to the total. For 1989, the last year Cuba benefited fully from Soviet economic support, the five-category total for the three-country composite was $8.7 billion, or about 50 percent higher than the corresponding $5.8 billion for Cuba.

Differences in the sectoral composition of foreign exchange receipts are even more striking. For the three-country composite,

Table 1.4
Cuba and the Three-Country Composite, General Indicators, 1990

Indicator	Costa Rica	Dominican Republic	Jamaica	Three-Country Composite	Cuba
Population (thousands)	3,111	7,384	2,489	12,984	10,732
Gross domestic product per capita ($ U.S.)	1,810	940	1,580	1,443	2,000[a]
Arable land (thousands of sq. km) Total	529	1,446	269	2,244	3,330
Sugar	39	206	40	285	1,350
Telephones (per 100 population)	9.7	3.0	5.0	5.9	2.0
Motor vehicles (per 100 population)	7.7	3.2	3.0	4.6	4.2
Energy consumption (kwh per capita)	980	580	1,030	863	1,530

Sources: For population, gross domestic product, telephones, energy consumption: Central Intelligence Agency (CIA), *The World Factbook* (Washington, D.C., 1992). For arable land: United Nations Food and Agriculture Organization (FAO), *The Production Yearbook 1991* (Rome, Italy, 1992). For motor vehicles: UN Statistical Office, *The UN Statistical Yearbook* (New York, 1988/1989), and Newspaper Enterprise Association, *World Almanac and Book of Facts* (New York, 1991).

[a] This figure is based on a greatly overvalued official exchange rate and thus overstates the level of per capita income.

Table 1.5
Cuba and the Three-Country Composite, Foreign Exchange Receipts, 1989
(in millions of U.S. dollars)

Category	Costa Rica	Dominican Republic	Jamaica	Three-Country Composite	Cuba
Total exports[a]	1,972	2,111	1,280	5,363	5,392
Manufactured exports to all OECD countries[b]	542	1,411	301	2,254	27
(Manufactured exports to the United States)	(514)	(1,178)	(280)	(1,972)	(0)
Sugar	13[c]	147[c]	38[c]	198	3,914[d]
Tourist expenditures[e]	207	750	593	1,550	240
Remittances[f]	39	306	300	645	100
Foreign direct investment[f]	95	110	57	267	50
Economic assistance	299	206	363	868	24
Official development assistance[g]	226	145	262	633	24
World Bank[h]	43	32	52	127	0
InterAmerican Development Bank[i]	30	29	49	108	0
Total All Categories	**2,612**	**3,483**	**2,593**	**8,693**	**5,806**

Sources:
[a] Data for Costa Rica, Dominican Republic, and Jamaica from International Monetary Fund (IMF), *Direction of Trade Statistics* (Washington, D.C., 1992). Data for Cuba from United Nations Economic Commission on Latin America and the Caribbean (ECLAC), *Economic Survey of Latin America and the Caribbean, 1989* (Santiago, Chile, 1991), 320.
[b] Organization for Economic Cooperation and Development (OECD), OECD Import-Export trade data microfiche (Paris, 1980, 1985, 1990).
[c] International Sugar Organization (ISO), *ISO Sugar Yearbook* (London, 1992).
[d] ECLAC, 1991.
[e] World Tourism Organization (WTO), *Yearbook of Tourism Statistics*, 2 vols. (Madrid, Spain, 1992).
[f] International Monetary Fund (IMF), *International Financial Statistics*, vol. 45 (Washington, D.C., 1991).
[g] OECD, Development Assistance Committee (DAC), *OECD Development Co-operation* (Paris, 1991). Bilateral Soviet aid is not included.
[h] World Bank, *World Debt Tables, 1991-1992*, Country Tables, vol. 2 (Washington, D.C., 1991).
[i] InterAmerican Development Bank, *Annual Report, 1989 and 1990* (Washington, D.C., 1989, 1990).

the largest categories of foreign exchange receipts are manufactured exports to OECD countries of $2.3 billion (of which 87
percent went to the United States); tourism expenditures of $1.6
billion; remittances from nationals living abroad, mostly in the
United States, of $0.6 billion; and development assistance of $0.9
billion. These four categories total $5.4 billion, or more than 60
percent of total listed foreign exchange receipts, while sugar
exports were only $0.2 billion, or 2 percent.

For Cuba, in contrast, $3.9 billion, or 67 percent, of total listed
foreign exchange receipts came from sugar exports, mostly to the
Soviet bloc at greatly inflated prices. The next highest category is
tourist expenditures at $240 million, while manufactured exports
to OECD countries and development assistance were insignifi-
cant, at $27 million and $24 million respectively. Remittances
from the more than 1 million Cubans living abroad are estimated
at roughly $100 million, or less than a sixth the level remitted to
the other three countries.[6]

Since 1989, economic expansion has continued generally
within the Caribbean Basin region, although at a somewhat sub-
dued rate because of the economic recession in the United States
and elsewhere. For the three-country composite, total foreign
exchange receipts for the categories listed in table 1.5 increased
from $8.7 billion in 1989 to $9.6 billion in 1990 and were probably in the $10 billion to $11 billion range by 1992. For Cuba, however, 1989 marked the abrupt turning point in its three-decade
economic dependence on the Soviet bloc. Foreign exchange
receipts, as explained in the next chapter, plummeted from $5.8
billion in 1989 to $2.7 billion by 1992, with severe negative
shocks throughout the economy.

A new Caribbean economic order has emerged from the
1980s, greatly transformed in its patterns of trade and investment,
more polarized on a regional basis, and moving steadily toward
even deeper interdependence. The adjustment process has some
disruptive economic consequences, but the broad prospect is one
of economic growth, job creation, and improved living standards.

At the very center of this regional activity, however, the largest
and most populous island nation, Cuba, remains almost totally dis-
engaged from its neighboring economic partners. The regional
economy, in fact, has the shape of a doughnut, to borrow the long-

standing analogy for the North Atlantic Treaty Organization (NATO) force structure without French participation. The NATO doughnut configuration prospered over the years, albeit at some budgetary cost, while France maintained greater freedom of action in its security relationships. The costs and benefits for Cuba, isolated at the center of the Caribbean economic doughnut, are far less favorable.

2
A Quantum Economic Setback for Castro

The cutoff of Soviet aid and the collapse of the Soviet bloc as even a market for commercial transactions have wreaked a devastating quantum setback to the Cuban economy and the Castro regime. The Cuban economy is estimated to have shrunk by 45 percent between 1989 and 1992, and an extremely acute foreign exchange crisis precludes early recovery.[1]

The financial crisis has two dimensions. One dimension is structural in nature, the need to reorient Cuban trade and other external economic transactions away from an 85 percent dependency on the former Soviet bloc and toward more market-oriented relationships. The three-decade experience with the Soviet bloc was one of managed economic distortion for political purposes. Cuba and the socialist economies of the East, 6,000 miles apart, were not natural trading partners, and trade was never based on demonstrated comparative advantage. Rather, Cuba would develop its annual list of priority import needs, which the Soviet Union and its allies would supply, receiving in return whatever the Cuban economy could usefully produce. Export and import pricing became an accounting procedure remote from actual costs. As a result, deeper and deeper distortions were built into the Cuban economy between what was being produced and what should be produced under market-competitive conditions. These distortions now need to be phased out, which will involve a fundamental restructuring of the national economy.

The deeply embedded distortions in the Cuban economy are most evident in the sugar sector. In 1959, the dominant role of sugar was denounced by the new revolutionary government as the strategy of "imperialist monopolies," and diversification to other agricultural and industrial products was a high economic priority. By the mid-1960s, however, sugar sales to the Soviet Union became the overriding priority, with greatly inflated export prices that reached more than eight times the world price in 1986.

Acreage devoted to sugar increased 33 percent between 1961 and 1987, while that devoted to corn declined by 52 percent. Moreover, the inflated Soviet purchase price for sugar enabled Cuba to avoid investment in new, more energy-efficient sugar mills even after the oil crises of the 1970s. Almost 90 percent of the 156 sugar mills in Cuba today were built before 1925, and production costs in 1992 are judged to be "way above" the world market price for sugar of less than 10 cents per pound. During the 1980s, while other sugar producers, from the Philippines to the Dominican Republic, were modernizing sugar mills to reduce energy costs and diversifying sugar land into other export crops, Cuba continued to put priority on ever-larger sugar production regardless of cost.[2]

The second, related dimension of the current financial crisis is the precipitous decline in foreign exchange available to finance imports, which not only has had severe negative impact on personal consumption but also effectively precludes the investment necessary to restructure the economy. Official Cuban statistics for trade and other external transactions are not available beyond 1989, the last year of full Soviet economic aid, and official statements of a general nature tend to understate, in some respects, the decline in recent economic performance. It is possible, however, to construct a reasonably accurate picture of Cuban external accounts through 1992 indirectly, through the statistics of Cuba's principal trading partners and from other sources.

Table 2.1 summarizes Cuban exports and other principal sources of foreign exchange from 1989 through 1992. For exports, the 1989 figures are official Cuban statistics. The figures for 1990 and 1991 are estimates based principally on the imports of Cuba's major trading partners, compiled by the U.S. Central Intelligence Agency (CIA),[3] and 1992 is a constructed figure, as explained below. Total exports were down only slightly from $5.4 billion in 1989 to $4.9 billion in 1990, more sharply to $3.6 billion in 1991, and then even more sharply to $2.2 billion in 1992. The total decline over the three-year period was 60 percent.

Sugar exports tell most of the story, with a 68 percent decline from $3.9 billion to $1.3 billion. The drop reflects primarily the termination of Soviet purchases at inflated prices, but sugar production also dropped by about 10 percent from 1991 to 1992 as a

Table 2.1
Cuban Foreign Exchange Receipts
(in millions of U.S. dollars)

Category	1989	1990	1991	1992
Total exports [a]	5,392	4,910	3,585	2,150
Sugar	3,914	3,645	2,575	1,250
Nickel	485	400	280	250
Citrus	139	150	120	110
Fish	127	125	130	120
Tobacco	85	110	95	90
Coffee	40	35	35	30
Medical products	58	100	50	50
Petroleum re-exports	213	45	25	0
Other	331	300	275	250
Tourist expenditures [b]	240	268	300	350
Remittances [c]	100	100	100	100
Foreign direct investment [c]	50	50	50	50
Economic assistance [d]	24	29	30	30
Total All Categories	**5,806**	**5,357**	**4,065**	**2,680**

Sources:

[a] All 1992 figures estimated as explained in text, except for sugar. Data for sugar from Central Intelligence Agency (CIA), *Cuba: Handbook of Trade Statistics (U)*, Directorate of Intelligence, Intelligence Research Paper (Washington, D.C., September 1992).

[b] World Tourism Organization, *Yearbook of Tourism Statistics*, 1989, 1990. 1991, 1992, estimated as explained in text.

[c] Estimated as explained in text.

[d] OECD, Development Assistance Committee (DAC), *OECD Development Co-operation* (Paris, 1989, 1990). Data for 1991, 1992 estimated as explained in text.

result of shortages of gasoline to run tractors, spare parts for maintenance of sugar mills, and fertilizers for the crop. The 1992 figure for sugar is based on 6.3 million tons of exports at a world market price of 9 cents per pound, which likely overstates export receipts somewhat because much of Cuban sugar is shipped long distances, for example, to the People's Republic of China (PRC) and Iran, and thus entails higher transportation costs and a lower net export price.[4] Nickel, the second largest category of exports, also declined sharply over the three-year period, by 48 percent, mostly because of a drop in world prices from the exceptionally high levels of 1988 and 1989, but quantities exported also fell because maintenance of antiquated Soviet equipment languished.

Medical products exports, stemming from the biotechnology initiative launched with great fanfare by the Castro government in 1986, show a decline from a high of $100 million in 1990 to an estimated $50 million in 1992. Despite the high hopes for burgeoning exports, as exemplified by predictions of several hundred million dollars of exports per year by the early 1990s, the commercial viability of Cuban biotechnology products apparently has not materialized. The most prominent export market publicly mentioned has been Brazil, and statistics on Brazilian imports from Cuba show $99 million for 1990, almost all for meningitis vaccine, dropping to $28 million in 1991. A Brazilian report in early 1992 concluded that the meningitis vaccine was only 54 percent effective and thus unreliable for use during epidemics, which makes further sales to Brazil doubtful.[5] There are several unconfirmed reports of small Cuban exports of biotechnology products in 1992, and the $50 million figure in table 2.1 is a rough estimate indicating relatively low sales.

Most other export categories are estimated as down slightly from 1991 levels based on shortages of fertilizers, spare parts for equipment, and gasoline and on the import figures of some of Cuba's principal trading partners for the first six to nine months of 1992. Re-exports of petroleum products, which earlier reflected surplus supplies of petroleum from the Soviet Union that Cuba re-exported at a profit, have now obviously ceased.

Among the other categories of foreign exchange receipts, the most important is tourism expenditures. The 1989 and 1990 figures of $240 million and $268 million are from the World Tourism

Table 2.2
Cuban Imports
(in millions of U.S. dollars)

Category	1989	1990	1991	1992	Percent decline 1989-1992
Food	1,011	840	720	600	41%
Raw materials	307	240	140	60	80
Petroleum	2,598	1,950	1,240	850	67
Chemical products	530	390	270	120	77
Machinery and equipment	2,531	2,380	820	350	86
Other manufactured goods	1,115	925	480	210	81
Other	32	20	20	10	69
Total Imports	**8,124**	**6,745**	**3,690**	**2,200**	**73%**

Source: Central Intelligence Agency (CIA), *Cuba: Handbook of Trade Statistics (U) 1989 – 1991* (Washington, D.C., 1992). Data for 1992 estimated as explained in text.

Organization annual reports, while the 1991 and 1992 estimates of $300 million and $350 million are explained in the next chapter. Remittances from overseas Cubans, mostly in the United States, are estimated at $100 million per year. Estimates range from less than $50 million per year, reflecting remittances officially reported to the U.S. Treasury under existing stringent regulations, to as high as $200 million, to include unrecorded transfers in currency and in goods such as clothing and medicine. The latter figure appears excessive in view of the recent tightening of U.S. Treasury regulations.

The foreign direct investment figure of $50 million per year is likely the most controversial in view of official Cuban statements about large foreign investment commitments, totaling hundreds of millions, if not billions, of dollars.[6] The admittedly rough estimate of $50 million, however, represents actual disbursements, not future commitments. This subject is also discussed in greater detail in the next chapter. Finally, economic assistance consists principally of relatively small contributions from UN agencies. The 1989 and 1990 assistance figures are from the OECD Development Assistance Committee, and later figures are estimated at a slightly higher level of $30 million per year.[7]

Total listed foreign exchange receipts, on the bottom line of table 2.1, show a decline from $5.8 billion in 1989 to $2.7 billion in 1992, a drop of 55 percent. This sharp decline is reflected in a corresponding drop in imports and, in fact, imports dropped even more precipitously. As shown in table 2.2, total imports declined from $8.1 billion in 1989 to only $2.2 billion in 1992, or by 73 percent. Again, the 1989 figures are Cuban statistics, while the figures for 1990 and 1991 are indirect estimates by the CIA based on the export figures of Cuba's principal trading partners and other trade reports. The 1992 import levels are based in part on statements by Fidel Castro and State Secretary Carlos Lage that total 1992 imports would be $2.2 billion, including 6.5 million tons of petroleum imports valued at $850 million.[8] Food imports for 1992 are estimated roughly at $600 million based on export figures for the first six to nine months of the year of some of Cuba's principal trading partners. Other import categories were reduced from the 1991 levels on a prorated basis in keeping with the $2.2 billion total figure.

The far sharper drop in imports compared with foreign exchange receipts is reflected in import levels for 1989 and 1990 $2.3 billion and $1.3 billion higher, respectively, than listed foreign exchange receipts for those years. The import level then drops below foreign exchange receipts by about $400 to $500 million in both 1991 and 1992. The earlier, higher import figures can be explained by additional forms of Soviet financial support that were not included in table 2.1, such as aid projects, expanded trade credits, and the hard currency spending of some 13,000 Soviet bloc advisers and their families.[9] Some trade credits were also extended by non-Communist countries, such as Mexico and Spain, but these have come to a virtual halt since Cuba ceased all service on its approximate $8 billion of debt to Western creditors.

The 1991 and 1992 import levels, substantially below estimated foreign exchange receipts, are more difficult to explain. The foreign exchange receipts estimates are not precise, and some categories, such as sugar exports and tourism expenditures, as already noted, may be on the high side. The Cuban government also continues to have relatively large official expenditures abroad, including extensive diplomatic missions, the prominent Cuban participation in the 1992 Olympic Games, and the July 1992 lavish trip to Spain by Fidel Castro with a large entourage. Another possible factor, conjectural at this point but consistent with the experience of the final phase of Soviet bloc communism, is that some hard currency earnings are being deposited abroad in anticipation of a collapse of the regime. The decentralized barter arrangements and accounting procedures that apparently prevail could make such political capital flight even more tempting.[10]

The sectoral breakdown of imports is particularly revealing with respect to the initial response of the Castro government to the financial crisis as well as to the longer-term consequences for the Cuban economy. Food imports show the smallest relative decline from 1989 to 1992 (41 percent), compared with the 73 percent decline for total imports. This reflects the political sensitivity of the shortages and food lines that have been reported extensively in the international press. Petroleum imports were also down by less than the average (67 percent) in the face of factory power shortages, residential blackouts, and disruption of public transportation. In both the food and petroleum sectors, the impact of reduced imports on the population is immediate, and although sharp cutbacks in supply have been unavoidable, the government has put priority on minimizing shortages in these sectors.

In contrast, the sharpest declines in imports have been in the categories of machinery and other manufactured goods, which constituted almost half of total imports in 1989 and which were reduced by 86 and 81 percent, respectively, by 1992. The cutback in these imports presents less immediate problems, except for the most critical spare parts that continue to be purchased on a cash basis. Machinery and other capital equipment imports are nevertheless essential for new investment projects as well as for maintenance of the existing industrial base and economic infrastructure. The adverse impact is longer-term and gradual, however, and therefore apparently of less immediate political concern to the Castro government.

In terms of the precipitous decline in imports caused by the termination of Soviet economic support, the year 1992 could mark a leveling off at the new low level, and in any event, the downward plunge was most severe in 1991 and, especially, 1992. The sharply lower levels of personal consumption and the power shortages, including the partial or total shutdown of many enterprises, can probably be held more or less at 1992 levels and should not worsen greatly in the immediate future. There could even be some improvement as the labor force is shifted toward achieving greater self-sufficiency in foodstuffs and other necessities, as explained in the following chapter.

This does not mean, however, that 1993 will bring about a new equilibrium and stabilization of the Cuban economy. The longer-term deterioration from a lack of capital equipment and other industrial and agricultural supplies is a cumulative process that threatens a progressive crumbling—or *desmoronamiento*—of the economic structure of the country in the broadest terms. Economic infrastructure for electric power, telecommunications, and transportation, consistently neglected, will gradually weaken all other economic activity and can take many years and large financial resources to reconstitute. Environmental degradation in Cuba, already serious in the sugar and nickel industries and acutely evident in Havana harbor, will worsen. The vaunted health care sector is experiencing shortages in medical supplies and equipment. Perhaps most threatened is the human resource base. Cuba has a highly educated labor force, well motivated and disciplined, according to most foreign observers. But the lack of jobs to match educational achievement, the growing unemployment, and the absence of consumer goods on which to spend one's salary all tend to undermine such motivation and discipline. Crime, corruption, and cynicism among the young are on the rise. The *desmoronamiento* of the human resource base could become, over time, the most damaging consequence of the ongoing financial crisis.

The Castro Reform Program

The visit of Soviet President Mikhail Gorbachev to Havana in April 1989 marked the beginning of the end for Soviet economic support to the Castro government. While the two leaders engaged in public pledges of harmony, Soviet trade officials, in private, were informing their Cuban counterparts that sugar export subsidies would be reduced and imports from the Soviet Union would have to be paid for in hard currency. A relatively generous interim trade agreement was reached for 1990, but in 1991 Soviet oil supplies were cut from 13 million to 10 million tons, and by 1992 the three-decade economic relationship with the now former Soviet Union had collapsed.

The Zero Option

Fidel Castro was quick to sense the impending crisis and, in true character, responded with dramatic force. In early 1990, he proclaimed the "special period for times of peace" and began preparations for the "zero option," meaning a zero level of Soviet economic assistance. Equally in character, however, the Castro response has been more an array of specific initiatives with some glaring inconsistencies than a coherent overall program for economic recovery.

The Castro zero-option response to the financial crisis has two very different components, one for Cubans producing for the domestic economy and the other for foreign companies as potential earners of foreign exchange. The domestic Cuban component is a radical restructuring of the economy toward economic self-sufficiency, or autarky, at a far more rudimentary level of economic development. Indeed, by all comparable standards, this economic program is one of *un*-development. Cuba has become an un-developing country. Bicycles are replacing automobiles. Horse-drawn carts are replacing delivery trucks. Oxen are replacing tractors. Factories are shut down and urban industrial workers resettled in rural areas to engage in labor-intensive agriculture. Food con-

sumption is shifting from meat and processed products to pota-
toes, bananas, and other staples.

This strategy of autarky and un-development, moreover, is
being carried forward within a rigid Communist framework of central planning and government ownership. Private enterprise, even
for small farms and home repair services, is forbidden and
denounced as sowing corruption and demoralization. The market
reform orientation of Soviet *perestroika* was viewed by the Castro
government as dangerously infectious to the Cuban work force,
and the reaction has been consistently unyielding. In 1989, the
popular general Arnaldo Ochoa, believed to be sympathetic to
perestroika thinking, was executed on unsubstantiated charges of
drug trafficking. At the Fourth Congress of Cuba's Communist
Party in October 1991, a grass-roots movement within the party
for limited market-oriented reforms was categorically rejected by
Fidel Castro and the harder-line ideologues.[1]

The second component of the Castro zero-option strategy has
been the active and highly publicized program to attract foreign
private investment so as to increase foreign exchange earnings.
The new investment laws are potentially far-reaching in legal content. Foreign investors can hold 50 percent or more equity participation in a number of sectors, including hotels, chemicals,
footwear, and textile assembly industry. The foreign company can
exercise a high degree of management control, including training,
hiring, and firing workers. Generous tax breaks are available, and
joint venture enterprises can be permitted to export and import
directly, free of customs duties, while retaining a share of foreign
exchange receipts.

The results thus far in attracting foreign investment, however,
have been disappointing. Only the tourism sector has shown clear
results, attracting substantial investment for hotels and support
services, although, as explained below, the outlook even in this
sector is unclear. In other targeted sectors, little new capital has
actually been invested in Cuba. Foreign businesspersons only dis-
cuss possible future commitments or engage in small service con-
tracts to position themselves for a post-Castro opening of the U.S.
market.

The extraordinary aspect of the Castro government's
courtship of foreign private companies is its stark contrast with

the government's vilification of private enterprise by Cubans, even for small-scale and family businesses. This constitutes a fundamental and irreconcilable contradiction for implementation of the Castro zero-option economic strategy. If foreign investors were to extend their scope of participation in the economy, such as through new investment for support services in the tourism sector and for large-scale employment of assembly industry workers, growing strains would be placed on the underfunded and retrogressive state sector, while if pervasive state controls and austerity continue to stultify the domestic economy, foreign private investment will be discouraged.

The overall zero-option strategy up to this point raises three interrelated questions, the answers to which will set the parameters for the future political as well as economic course of the Castro government: (1) the sustainability of the current low level of personal consumption, (2) the ability to increase foreign exchange earnings over the next several years, and (3) the medium- to long-term impact of structural deterioration.

Sustaining the Low Level of Personal Consumption

The hardships and humiliation of the Cuban people, who must spend long hours in lines for severely rationed food, clothing, and other necessities, could become a flash point for political upheaval against the Castro regime, but it has not yet, in itself, appeared to pose a serious security threat to the government. Food is scarce and of poor quality by traditional Cuban standards, but there is no likelihood of starvation, and malnutrition is thus far of limited scope. The life-threatening climate of former Soviet Union and Yugoslav winters is also absent from tropical Cuba. Personal consumption levels in Cuba may, in fact, be higher than would appear from empty store shelves and could improve somewhat from what was probably their nadir in 1992. A black market for food and other consumer goods constitutes a supplement to meager official supplies. Family gardens in the countryside can provide relief to urban friends and relatives. The forceful government policy of higher food self-sufficiency, however primitive the methods, is also producing results that should alleviate shortages for some food staples.

In sum, the less than life-threatening shortages, together with

Table 3.1
Projected Foreign Exchange Receipts under the Castro Reform Program
(in millions of U.S. dollars)

Category (% yearly change)	1992	1995 Projections	
		Low	High
Total exports	2,150	1,718	2,113
Sugar (-10%/-5%)	1,250	911	1,072
Nickel (0%/+5%)	250	250	289
Other exports (-5%/+5%)	650	557	752
Tourist expenditures (+5%/+20%)	350	405	605
Remittances (0%/0%)	100	100	100
Foreign direct investment (0%/0%)	50	50	50
Economic assistance (0%/0%)	30	30	30
Total All Categories	2,680	2,303	2,898

Source: 1992 data from table 2.1. 1995 projections estimated as explained in text.

the harsh and omnipresent security forces, have inhibited widespread popular protest over the sharp deterioration in the standard of living. The new low level of personal consumption is probably sustainable as long as the political cohesion of the government and the security forces prevails, which depends on the second and third questions.

Increasing Foreign Exchange Earnings

Although shortages may be bearable in the short term, the Castro economic strategy is at a dead end if it cannot demonstrate that, over the next several years, foreign exchange earnings can be increased substantially, thereby enabling a gradual improvement in living standards and the creation of new jobs through investment. Under current circumstances, however, the prospect for such an increase over the next several years is virtually nil.

Table 3.1 projects Cuban foreign exchange earnings through 1995. The 1992 level of $2.7 billion is taken from table 2.1, and the out years are projected as a range based on high and low estimates. The resulting levels for 1995 show a high of $2.9 billion and a low of $2.3 billion, or, in other words, no significant change from 1992. This implies that the import level will also remain down at about the $2.2 billion level of 1992, with severely reduced imports not only of foodstuffs and petroleum but even more so of machinery, equipment, and other industrial and agricultural inputs.

The projections in table 3.1 are based primarily on estimates for sugar, nickel, and tourism, which account for almost two-thirds of the total. Sugar is most important, and the 10 percent decline in production in 1992 will almost certainly be followed by further declines over the next several years. In September 1992, the Cuban minister for sugar, Juan Herrera, warned that the 1992 – 1993 harvest would be even more difficult than the previous year.[2] Shortages of fertilizer, gasoline for tractors, and spare parts for sugar mills will have cumulative negative impact. Extensive delays in the harvest schedule, as happened in 1992, slow planting for the following year. The high projection in table 3.1 incorporates a further 5 percent annual decline in sugar production, and the low projection a 10 percent annual decline.

Nickel production is projected in a range of 5 percent annual

growth—reaching 40,000 metric tons in 1995—to zero growth—
maintaining the estimated 1992 level of 34,500 metric tons. The
1992 world price is maintained through 1995, which could be
optimistic because there is currently, and likely to continue over
the next several years, a downward pressure on world prices from
increased Russian exports of nickel, made available as the Russian
domestic consumption of nickel declines with overall industrial
production. Major new foreign investment in Cuba for nickel production will almost certainly not take place, despite earlier optimistic reports, although some upgrading of existing facilities could
result in a modest increase in production as provided in the high
projection.[3]

Tourism is the most difficult sector to project because the
actual situation is very uncertain and hard facts are in short supply. New and refurbished hotel rooms, including foreign investment by Spanish, Jamaican, and other companies, increased
capacity from 10,300 rooms in 1989 to approximately 13,000
rooms in 1992. Hotel building has apparently slowed down, however, in the face of lower-than-hoped-for occupancy levels, which
may be as low as 50 percent on average compared with an average
70 percent annual occupancy elsewhere in the Caribbean. The
earlier target of 30,000 rooms by 1996 will not be reached and
will probably be much lower. A related uncertainty concerns the
number of visitors. Despite active marketing in Europe, Canada,
and elsewhere, many tourists return from Cuba with negative
accounts of poor food and services as well as discomfort over the
political tensions created by "tourist apartheid," whereby hotels
and restaurants for foreign tourists are isolated from the local population. The official estimated level of 500,000 visitors in 1992 is
used for the projections here, but the final count may turn out to
be lower.[4]

The most difficult calculation is for tourist expenditures.
Official Cuban data for the period 1986 – 1988 show average
expenditure by Western visitors to Cuba of $460 to $480, compared with $750 elsewhere in the Caribbean. This difference
reflects the facts that most Cuban hotels have a relatively low
quality of service and that the large majority of European and
other tourists come on low-price budget packages. A week-long
vacation trip to Cuba from Cancun costs only $500, including

hotel, meals, and airfare. An average $500 expenditure in Cuba for 500,000 visitors would thus result in a total expenditure estimate of $250 million. A report based on conversations with a Cuban official, however, produced an expenditure figure for 1992 of $445 million, implying average expenditure of $890 per visitor, well above the average elsewhere in the Caribbean. The figure used here for 1992 of $350 million total expenditure essentially splits the difference and is considered to be on the high side.[5] The projections for the rate of growth in visitor expenditures through 1995 are for a high of 20 percent, reflecting optimistic Cuban expectations, and a low of 5 percent. As described in chapter 1, growth in tourism expenditures for the Caribbean region was 12 percent from 1985 to 1990, and the current slow economic growth or recession in Europe and North America could lower that figure over the next year or two.

The critical conclusion, in any event, is that even with this wide range of growth projections for tourism, the growth in revenues is only $50 million to $250 million by 1995, or very small compared with the massive $6 billion decline in imports since 1989. Moreover, tourism is the only clearly positive component in the overall foreign exchange earning outlook for Cuba.

All other exports are projected to grow at plus 5 to minus 5 percent annually, reflecting offsetting forces at play. The high priority the Castro government gives to generating export earnings should produce increases for some products, while the progressive deterioration of the industrial base and shortages of imported components will tend to reduce exports for others. In any event, exports other than sugar and nickel totaled only $650 million in 1992, and the projected range for 1995 is plus or minus about $100 million.

The remaining items in table 3.1 are projected out at 1992 levels. A special note is in order with respect to foreign direct investment, which is estimated at $50 million per year through 1995. This is a rough estimate, because no comprehensive figures are available on actual foreign exchange inflows for investment, and is perhaps optimistic. The largest investments by far have been for hotels, but a $30 million hotel will likely involve foreign funding of about 50 percent, or $15 million, for imported materials and equipment, spread over three years of construction, or roughly $5 million per year. Even if six to eight hotels were in full-scale construction, which is apparently not now the case, this would generate an annual investment inflow of only $30 million to $40 million. Another reported investment is for a $40 million to $65 million joint venture with the Italian firm ITALCABLE for telecommunications infrastructure for the hotel sector, but there has been no indication of the extent to which the project has been implemented.[6] The next largest reported investment is for $10 million by the French oil company Total for oil exploration, which is not being continued.[7] The $50 million level should thus be considered a reasonable order of magnitude and is certainly far below the very large figures of hundreds of millions, if not billions, of dollars of reported commitments that will almost certainly not be realized over the next few years.

The bottom line for the 1995 foreign exchange receipts projection is that little if any relief from the severe squeeze on imports will be forthcoming under current circumstances, and thus there will be no improvement for at least several years in the harsh and depressed state of the Cuban economy. The outlook becomes even more bleak when considering the cumulative structural deterioration under way in the Cuban economy.

The Impact of Structural Deterioration on the Economy

The cumulative process of structural deterioration in the Cuban economy is the least visible or quantifiable of the three questions addressed here, but it can ultimately have the greatest medium- to long-term adverse consequences. The progressive negative impact on economic infrastructure, industrial capacity, education and health services, and the human resource base generally has already been described. The near total halt in new investment projects and neglect of maintenance of existing facilities, except in the hotel sector, are at present causing such economic deterioration throughout the national economy.

This longer-term dilemma from short-term financial crisis is not unique to Cuba. Other countries, from Russia to Zaire to neighboring Haiti, are currently experiencing serious structural deterioration in their economies as well. Cuba stands out, however, for the abruptness of the change and the severity of the economic setback. Even in the beleaguered Russian economy, imports declined by only 55 percent from 1990 to 1992 and are projected by the World Bank to increase in 1993, compared with the 73 percent drop in Cuban imports thus far. Moreover, most other economically troubled nations are engaged in dialogue with the international financial community to develop the means for recovery and are receiving various forms of trade credits and other financial assistance from it. In contrast, the Cuban government stands defiantly alone, with no feasible short- or medium-term strategy to reverse the process of decline, while actuarial tables indicate more than 10 years of further life for the Castro-led government.

The other unique feature of the current Cuban economic dilemma is the trade embargo imposed by the United States, Cuba's natural and potentially dominant trading partner. The zero-option economic strategy of the Castro government has been critiqued up to this point for its retrogressive domestic program and its inner contradictions with regard to attracting foreign investment but with the proviso "under current circumstances," which would include a continuance of the U.S. embargo. The circumstances under which the embargo might be lifted are essentially political in character, and the probability of such an act by the U.S. government while Castro's Communist regime is still in control is extremely low. Nevertheless, in the context of this study, it is relevant to consider the economic consequences of an early lifting of the embargo on the Castro zero-option strategy.

The U.S. Embargo Dimension

Whether the United States should lift the trade embargo on Cuba now that the cold war is over and Fidel Castro no longer poses a security threat to the United States is a divisive issue. Foreign governments, from Mexico and Venezuela to European NATO allies, advise the United States to lift the embargo now. So do foreign business interests recently established in Cuba, which stand to benefit when the U.S. market is reopened, as well as a growing number of U.S. businesspersons who are disadvantaged when, for example, foreign hotel companies acquire prime beachfront properties. Some U.S. Latin America experts also recommend an early lifting of the embargo while the Castro government is still in place.[8] All or almost all members of the U.S. Congress, in con-

trast, support a continued embargo, and the congressionally initi-
ated Cuban Democracy Act of 1992 tightened the embargo by prohibiting U.S. subsidiaries in third countries from trading with
Cuba. Presidential candidate Bill Clinton supported the 1992 act
as did President George Bush after initial opposition.[9] The politically active Cuban-American community overwhelmingly supports retention of the embargo until the Castro regime collapses.

In this polarized context, those favoring a continued embargo
argue that raising it would provide financial benefits to Fidel
Castro and thus a new lease on life for his troubled regime, while
those opposed contend that more open trade would pressure
Castro to undertake further reforms and an earlier transition to
democratic government. In fact, both of these effects would be set
in motion, but there has been little attempt, either within governments or by private research institutions, to sort out what actually
might happen in such circumstances. Much would depend on how
and in what form the embargo was lifted.

The projected scenario that follows can be considered the
minimal level of actions on both sides for an early lifting of the
embargo. On the Cuban side, no basic change in the current political system or economic program is assumed, but Castro would
almost certainly have to make some significant political moves,
probably in the area of human rights, such as releasing political
prisoners and easing police repression of dissidents. There would
also be some mutual diplomatic steps, such as opening discussion
on the issue of expropriation claims by U.S. citizens and, perhaps,
the reestablishment of full diplomatic relations. The significance
of such political steps for a lifting of the embargo is not their substantive content but, rather, the positive change that would result
in the political atmosphere, which would have a corresponding
positive impact on the investment climate in Cuba as expecta-
tions rose for further steps to open Cuba to trade and investment
with the United States.

As for the form of lifting the embargo, the initial action is likely to be limited to ending the prohibition on trade and travel and
would not include the granting of most-favored-nation (MFN) tariff
treatment or generalized tariff preferences and other even more
generous access to the U.S. market under the Caribbean Basin
Initiative. Investment insurance against political risk, as provided

by the Overseas Private Investment Corporation (OPIC), and economic assistance from the United States or multilateral development banks would also be withheld pending further steps on the Cuban side.

Yet even under these initial, limiting circumstances, the immediate financial benefits to the Castro government would be very substantial and would come from several distinct sources. Much of the limited foreign exchange currently available for imports—the $2.2 billion level in 1992—would be shifted from imports from European and other sources to U.S. suppliers, presumably at significantly lower prices because of the proximity of these suppliers and the more competitive prices offered. If a third of total imports were shifted in this way at an average saving of 15 percent, a net saving in the order of $100 million would accrue to the Castro government. U.S. exporters would also, of course, benefit in the process.

The more important benefits for Cuba, however, would derive from the lifting of travel and currency restraints for U.S. citizens and the resulting tourism expenditures and increases in remittances by Cuban Americans to relatives in Cuba. Travel to Cuba by visiting Cuban Americans, businesspersons, and U.S. tourists more generally would surge. Existing hotel capacity could increase occupancy rates by up to 50 percent, average room rates could increase by a third, and cruise ships would quickly reschedule itineraries to include Havana or Varadero Beach. The anticipated impact on tourism from a reopened Cuba is described in greater detail in chapter 5, and the related estimate in this limited opening context is that visitor expenditures could increase $300 to $400 million per year almost immediately.[10]

The increase in remittances from Cuban Americans to relatives in Cuba could have similar impact. The current estimated level of $100 million per year could easily increase by $200 to $300 million per year, based on the level of remittances that normally flow back to other Caribbean nations such as Jamaica and the Dominican Republic. Indeed, as also discussed in chapter 5, the remittance level to a fully restructured and democratic Cuba would be on the order of $700 million to $800 million dollars per year. The Castro government, however, currently appropriates most of the officially remitted dollars by imposing a greatly overvalued exchange rate for the peso, which would likely deter much of the remittance flow.

The impact of lifting the U.S. embargo on Cuban exports to the United States and new foreign investment in Cuba would probably be more modest during an initial period. High U.S. tariffs, in the absence of MFN and tariff preferences, would constitute a major competitive disadvantage for Cuba vis-à-vis other Caribbean exporters of manufactured goods and many agricultural products. A few commodities, however, such as nickel, coffee, pineapples, and bananas, would face low or nil tariffs even without MFN, while some U.S. as well as other foreign investors would likely be willing to take the risk of investing in Cuba in anticipation of further actions to improve access to the U.S. market. A rough estimate of $100 to $200 million per year from both new exports and foreign investment would appear reasonable if not conservative.

Taken together, these various initial responses to a lifting of the U.S. embargo, even in the minimal circumstances posited here, would result in an increase in foreign exchange receipts of $700 million to $1.0 billion per year, or roughly one-third to one-half higher than the current depressed level. This additional hard currency would enable the Castro government, in turn, to alleviate acute food and fuel shortages and to give some relief to industries in need of spare parts and industrial inputs. A substantial increase in actual foreign investment, especially in export-oriented industries, would lend support to the government view that the limited reform program could work over time. The Castro regime would indeed have a new lease on life.

The new lease on life would not be static, however, and the pressures to extend reforms and loosen central control over the economy would grow. This second effect cannot be quantified, and much would depend on the political debate that would ensue within the Castro regime over the issue of resisting or acquiescing in the momentum that would build for further change. Within the tourism sector alone there would be great pressure to liberalize support services to cope with rapidly growing demand. Pervasive personal contact with U.S. businesspersons interested in investing in Cuba would focus on the need to take the necessary political steps to obtain MFN treatment and trade preferences. Likely initial dialogue with the international financial institutions, incipient bilateral aid programs from donor countries other than the United States, and requests from many private voluntary organizations to establish grass-roots development assistance projects in Cuba would all contribute to the pressures for more far-reaching reform. Foreign private enterprises that employ Cuban managers and workers at premium wages, as is already happening in foreign-owned hotels, would become role models.

A precise course and time frame for this minimum-level scenario for raising the embargo is not possible to predict, but it would tend in one of two directions. One direction would be a prolonged entrenchment of hard-line Communist rule, whereby foreign exchange inflows from the United States would help sustain political control while broader economic reforms were resisted and internal growth languished. This would be the worst of all possible outcomes and could well end, after extended downward drift in the economy, in violent confrontation. The other direction would be a further opening and liberalization of the Cuban economy. The likelihood of this latter course, either through an early lifting of the embargo or any alternative sequence of events, would be influenced by perceptions within Cuba as to what would happen in the event of radical change toward a market-oriented economy, which is the subject of the next two chapters.

4
Cuba Restructured: The Political Assumption

Fidel Castro has stated on various occasions that a radical market-oriented restructuring of Cuba would cause economic collapse and chaos as is happening in Russia. The most important conclusion of this study is that such a statement is totally unfounded. A restructured Cuba would have some parallels with the experience of the former Soviet Union, as well as some lessons to be learned from it, but the circumstances currently facing Cuba differ greatly from those of the former Soviet Union in key respects, almost all favorable to Cuba. The most important difference is that Cuba is situated at the center of the Caribbean regional economy. Contrary to the dire Castro prediction, an early and highly positive response from transition to a market economy is eminently feasible for Cuba.

A projection is made here for the response of the Cuban economy to a fundamental market-oriented restructuring in conjunction with a lifting of the U.S. embargo. The projection is for a five-year period, beginning at the time the embargo is lifted, and is referred to as "Cuba restructured plus five," or "CR plus five," for short. Because the economic projection needs to be based on assumptions about an accompanying political transition, however, the political transition is addressed first. There is, in fact, an interaction between the paths of political and economic change. Reasonably favorable political circumstances are prerequisite for a successful economic restructuring, while a clear prospect of economic success will tend to encourage the necessary political change. In this latter sense, the CR plus five projection will, it is hoped, convey an element of self-fulfilling prophecy.

The political assumption is for a two-stage transition to democratic government, as explained below.[1] This assumed course is not a "most likely" prediction but, rather, a normative statement as to an optimistic yet realistic course of events. Underlying the assumption is the need for a spirit of reconciliation both within

36

Cuba and across the Florida Straits with Cuban-American expatri-ates—the spirit of cultivating a white rose, as expressed by José Martí. More explicitly, the political assumption would preclude a negative course of prolonged instability and violence, perhaps even civil war, which would not only retard the economic transi-tion but would poison political and social relationships over a much longer period, with corresponding negative impact on the investment climate and economic recovery more broadly.

The first stage of democratic transition is assumed to run for a period of up to two years and would be a rather confused and tense period of organizing the return to elected government and implementing the first steps of economic reform. Some form of interim government, broadly representative of the people and based on the need for reconciliation, would be charged with con-stitutional reform leading to free and open elections. An elected constituent assembly, or *constituyente*, with a mandate to draw up a new constitution, could be part of the process. Internation-ally observed presidential and legislative elections would follow at the end of this first stage.

The second stage, comprising years three to five of the eco-nomic projection, would proceed under the duly elected govern-ment. Again, a degree of confusion and discord can be anticipated for a new democratically elected government after more than three decades of nondemocratic rule. The assumption here is not for outstanding or even very good performance but, rather, a mini-mum ability to carry forward the basic restructuring of the econo-my, as explained in greater detail below, while maintaining domes-tic peace and reasonable tranquility. The newly elected government would engage with the international financial institu-tions for technical assistance to carry out economic reforms as well as for mobilizing official development finance and private investment. The relationship with the United States is assumed to be very positive.

Lessons Learned from Eastern Europe

Further specification is necessary about initial steps that the gov-ernment can and should take for transition to a market economy, particularly during the initial two-year stage. The experience of Eastern Europe since 1989 has relevance, to varying degrees, in each of four priority areas—international financial institutions, private property rights, infrastructure, and foreign debt—that would need to be addressed.

Relations with International Financial Institutions

The earliest possible contact with the international financial institutions—the International Monetary Fund (IMF), the World Bank, and the InterAmerican Development Bank (IDB)—is an important step. Technical assistance from these institutions, together with that from other governments and the private sector, will be critical for creating the institutional framework for a market economy, including financial services, investment laws and regulations, and private property rights. Also, membership in these institutions should come as early as possible, first in the IMF, as prerequisite for participation in the development banks. IMF membership will require presentation of coherent fiscal, monetary, and international financial programs, worked out in advance with Fund staff, which can, in itself, be a valuable learning process. Membership in the development banks will make Cuba eligible for substantial long-term project and other financing.

Establishment of Private Property Rights

Early establishment of private property rights is essential for transition to a market economy, and privatization in key sectors, including tourism, the service sector more broadly, construction, and small- to medium-scale agriculture, should get early attention. These are the sectors that can provide the quickest response in employment, food supplies, and foreign exchange earnings, as demonstrated, for example, in Poland. Privatization of larger state enterprises, such as those for sugar, mining, and petroleum, will be more complicated and politically sensitive and would probably be left to the second stage of constitutionally elected government.

The issue of private property rights is linked to expropriation claims by Cubans and U.S. citizens, the latter totaling about $5.5 billion. Based on the experience of Eastern Europe, a general approach of compensation rather than restitution would be more expeditious and would alleviate fears within Cuba of people being dispossessed from their homes. The approach for some industrial and agricultural enterprises, however, could be tailored so as to give special bidding status to former owners during the privatization procedure.

An early understanding on expropriation claims by U.S. citizens is important, among other things, because it is a precondition for the provision of U.S. economic assistance. Such an understanding would have to take account of agreements reached by the Castro government on expropriation claims of other third country nationals as well as any overlapping property rights from recent joint ventures with foreign firms undertaken by the Castro government.

Priorities for Infrastructure

A restructured private sector will face many needs for economic infrastructure, especially in the transportation, telecommunications, and power generation sectors. At the outset, the development banks will play a key role, together with bilateral aid donors and the private sector, in the financing of such infrastructure projects. The inevitable confusion during the initial period, and needs that will far exceed available financing, however, will make the establishment of priorities for such infrastructure project financing a critical area of decision making. The Cuban government will have a unique opportunity to begin anew in building a modern infrastructure for its economy, but it must make the right decisions with respect to first-priority needs, most appropriate technologies, and environmentally beneficial results. This is an issue that Russia and the other former Soviet republics have not yet fully addressed.

Foreign Debt

Foreign debt is a most fluid issue with respect to transition from a Communist to a democratic, market-oriented government. Poland was able to negotiate a 50 percent write-down of its official foreign debt, while Russia thus far has sought a five-year moratorium on servicing debt incurred prior to democratization. No former Communist country has yet formally stated its wish or intent to repudiate debt of the earlier Communist regime. Negotiations elsewhere in Latin America to reduce and restructure external debt, under the Brady plan, are also relevant, with Costa Rica, for example, having negotiated an effective 70 percent to 80 percent reduction in its foreign debt.

In this context, Cuba has an $8 billion debt with Western creditors, none of which is with the United States, and an estimated 15 billion to 20 billion ruble debt with the former Soviet Union. None of this foreign debt has been serviced by the Castro government in recent years. The Soviet debt is apparently denominated in rubles, which would make its market value as of late 1992 less than $100 million.

At this stage, the best that can be said is that the Cuban economic transition team should include nimble debt negotiators who will keep abreast of precedents elsewhere in the former Communist world. A moratorium on debt servicing for at least the first two or three years of transition would be a reasonable starting point.

Invidious Comparison with the Former Soviet Union

In addition to lesson-learning parallels with the East European experience, there are even more important contrasts that would face a restructured Cuba. Five such contrasts stand out, in each case to the great comparative advantage of Cuba.

The Industrial Dinosaurs

The massive and greatly overstaffed industrial and defense production complexes in the former Soviet Union, and to a lesser extent in Poland, constitute the most intractable obstacle to market-oriented reforms in those formerly Communist countries. The Russian defense complex alone employs 10 million workers and has high regional intensity. The city of Nizhny Novgorod, for example, has 450 defense plants. Attempts to convert these obsolete "dinosaur" industries to commercially competitive enterprises are largely futile. Closing them down, however, would throw millions of people out of work, which is deemed politically unacceptable, so thousands of state enterprises continue to operate with huge government subsidies, producing products that nobody wants to buy.

The situation in Cuba appears far less grave in relative terms. State heavy industry and military production play a smaller role in the economy. The main Cuban steel complex at Antillana de

Acero employed only 7,000 workers before recent layoffs. Some industrial facilities, such as cement and fertilizer plants, should be convertible to profitable private production. In any event, 60 percent to 70 percent of industrial plants have reportedly been shut down, partially or fully, and the workers discharged, under the Castro zero-option autarky program.[2] Labor reabsorption through new manufacturing and service industries should also be easier because Cuban dinosaur industries have lower regional concentration than the former Soviet Union's, while labor mobility is higher within the relatively small island.

The Unemployed Military

The more than 3 million personnel of the former Soviet armed forces present a dilemma for Russia similar to its dinosaur industries. The budget cost of maintaining such forces is crushing, while the cutbacks in personnel thus far have created enormous problems in the absence of civilian jobs and housing for those discharged. The return to Russia of several hundred thousand troops based in Eastern Europe and elsewhere poses especially acute housing problems. Loss of prestige and economic hardships for the officer corps could develop into a political threat to the fledgling democratic government in Moscow.

Cuba also has a large military establishment for a country with fewer than 11 million people: an army of 145,000, a navy of 14,000, and an air force of 22,000.[3] The absorption of sharp cutbacks in military spending and personnel could be much easier in Cuba than in Russia, however, if managed properly. A reintegration of Cuba into the Caribbean regional economy would create very substantial civilian employment opportunities for Cuban air force and navy personnel. Civil passenger and air freight traffic, particularly to the United States, would expand rapidly, presumably including a major share for Cuban airlines. Similar growth would emerge for maritime traffic, including cruise lines, auto ferries, and all classes of cargo and fishing vessels, with corresponding needs for port facilities and ship maintenance. Trained Cuban air force and navy personnel should need little encouragement to move into these expanding job markets.

The Cuban army is much larger and would likely require more targeted assistance to facilitate transition to private-sector employment. Nevertheless, the officer corps and noncommissioned technicians are generally well trained and educated and thus potentially valuable as managers and skilled workers. As discussed in the appendix, U.S. foreign assistance to a restructured Cuba should place priority on the retraining of military personnel, with linkages to U.S. business schools and vocational training centers.

The Fiscal Hemorrhage

Russian inflation exceeded 1,000 percent in 1992 and could spiral even higher in 1993 unless the fiscal deficit of up to 20 percent of gross domestic product is greatly reduced. The alternative of uncontrolled inflation financed by the Central Bank printing press will inevitably lead to the collapse of the Russian reform program—sooner rather than later. The principal causes of the Russian fiscal deficit/hyperinflation dilemma, however, are the two preceding issues: the industrial dinosaurs and the unemployed army.

A noninflationary fiscal program during the initial stage of Cuban restructuring will be a central and immediate challenge for whatever government is in place. Nothing focuses the official mind more than the need to draw up financial accounts that are in reasonable balance. Financial management under the Castro government apparently has been in considerable disorder, and thus the new fiscal accounts will have to be developed largely from scratch. IMF and other foreign technical assistance will play an important role in this central task.

The fiscal challenge for a restructured Cuba in comparison with that facing Russia, however, will be much less daunting to the extent that subsidies to state enterprises and military expenditures can be rapidly reduced. As explained above, this would be far more manageable in Cuba than is currently the case in Russia.

Environmental Degradation

The former Soviet Union faces overwhelming environmental problems. In the energy sector, dangerously unsafe nuclear reactors could cost tens of billions of dollars to replace or make safer, while low-quality, coal-generated electricity pollutes the atmosphere. Lakes and rivers are highly poisoned, causing severe health risks. Large industrial complexes combine all of the above in concentrated environmental disaster areas.

Cuba also has major environmental problems. Havana's harbor is highly contaminated from industrial, maritime, and urban waste disposal. The sugar, nickel, and paper industries are polluting rivers and coastal waters. Air pollution at cement plants and other industrial sites is serious. The nuclear power plant under construction at Juragua would likely be unsafe if completed, while planned peat exploitation in swamp lands for power generation would cause wide-ranging environmental degradation.[4]

The difference for Cuba, however, is that its environmental problems are not as extensive or far advanced as those in Russia, and they are more amenable to remedial action. New private investment together with financial resources from the multilateral development banks could be mobilized relatively quickly to stem and reverse the problems enumerated here.

Absence of an Export Strategy

Russia and the other former Soviet republics have no apparent export strategy for short- to medium-term economic recovery. Petroleum and natural gas exports accounted for two-thirds of former Soviet export revenues, and production of these products is declining, with little hope of a turnaround for at least several years. Most other former Soviet exports went to other Communist countries or were based on noneconomic barter arrangements with developing countries. Very few of these products are now commercially competitive. The former Soviet Union also does not have a natural or regional export market to develop. The European Community (EC) is a closed market for agricultural products and gives preferences to its members, which should soon include the Czech Republic, Hungary, Poland, and Slovakia but not Russia and other former Soviet republics.

Cuba, in contrast, is at the center of the new Caribbean economic order, with immediate prospects for a surge in job-creating investment and foreign exchange earnings once market forces are unleashed and the U.S. market is reopened. This is by far Cuba's greatest advantage in comparison with the former Soviet Union, although it is also the most controversial and the least clearly understood. Fidel Castro has repeatedly denied that it even exists. A Cuban export-oriented economic strategy would have a number of distinct facets that need careful examination in the context of the Caribbean regional economy of the 1990s. The conclusion drawn here, as will be seen, is decidedly optimistic for a restructured Cuba.

5
The Cuba Restructured Plus Five Projection

A five-year projection—the Cuba restructured or "CR plus five" projection—has been made for the Cuban economy based on the foregoing political assumption. The projection is again principally in terms of foreign exchange receipts, which will constitute the driving force for broader economic growth. Increased foreign exchange enables a higher level of imports, which leads, in turn, to still higher levels of investment and job creation. In this sense, it is an export-oriented strategy in keeping with the concept underlying the Caribbean Basin Initiative of the 1980s. Indeed, a restructured Cuba should become the outstanding success story for what the CBI was meant to achieve.

The initial year of the five-year period is not specified. Instead, the projection simply begins at the point when the United States lifts the embargo and grants MFN status to Cuba and Cuba begins comprehensive restructuring to a market economy. What the beginning phase of such restructuring would mean in more specific terms was explained, in part, in the preceding chapter's discussion of lessons learned from Eastern Europe and is elaborated further in the sector-by-sector discussion of the projection below. Except when otherwise specified, the projection is based on 1992 prices and levels of national income and therefore does not reflect increases in dollar values over the five-year period resulting from inflation and income-generated market growth.

The projection is an aggregate of 15 components that together come close to the total foreign exchange inflow available to the Cuban economy. The projections for some of the components (exports of sugar, nickel, and fish) are based principally on existing conditions within Cuba. Other projected components (assembly industry, remittances, economic aid, and foreign direct investment) are derived in large part from recent experience elsewhere in the Caribbean region, while still others (tourism and nontraditional agriculture) draw on both internal Cuban and regional mar-

Table 5-1
The CR Plus Five Projection
(in millions of U.S. dollars)

Source of Foreign Exchange Receipts	1992	Cuba Restructured Plus Five (year)				
		1	2	3	4	5
Exports of Goods	2,150	2,200	2,490	2,910	3,550	4,270
Sugar	1,250	1,200	1,250	1,300	1,400	1,500
Other agriculture	330	360	450	550	650	800
Fish	120	130	150	170	190	220
Nickel	250	300	350	400	450	500
Other mining	10	10	20	50	100	150
Manufactures (mostly assembly industry)	100	100	150	300	600	900
Other	90	100	120	140	160	200
Services	350	900	1,225	1,600	2,025	2,500
Hotel visitors	350	800	1,000	1,200	1,400	1,600
Cruise ships	0	50	75	100	125	150
Residential construction for nonresidents	0	0	50	150	300	500
Other service	0	50	100	150	200	250
Foreign direct investment	50	100	200	400	600	800
Remittances	100	800	800	700	700	700
Economic assistance	30	100	300	600	800	700
Official export credits	0	300	500	500	500	500
Total All Categories	2,680	4,400	5,515	6,710	8,175	9,470

Source: As explained in text.

ket conditions. A few components (services other than tourism and residential construction for nonresidents) have no quantifiable comparative measure and are projected on what are believed to be reasonable yet conservative estimates.

Such five-year projections under greatly changed political as well as economic circumstances within Cuba are not meant to be precise. As described in the sector-by-sector discussion, however, the rough orders of magnitude are highly plausible, and the relative magnitudes and differing growth paths among the components over the five-year period are reasonably well established. Most important, the central conclusion of the projection is clearly substantiated, namely, that the Cuban economy can be transformed in a relatively short time into one of high economic growth and job creation, increasingly integrated with the North American/Caribbean region.

The CR plus five projection is presented in table 5.1. The bottom line of total foreign exchange receipts, which was earlier estimated at $2.7 billion in 1992, rises sharply to $4.4 billion in the first year of restructuring and then progressively up to $9.5 billion in the fifth and final year. This represents an extraordinary three- to fourfold increase from the depressed 1992 level and contrasts sharply with the virtually flat projection out to 1995 for the current Castro reform program. The approximate $9 billion to $10 billion level at the end of five years is substantially higher than the 1989 level when Soviet aid was still in full bloom and is of comparable magnitude to that of the three-country composite total for Costa Rica, the Dominican Republic, and Jamaica, estimated at $9.2 billion in 1990.

The projection also highlights the contrasts in the relative importance of the components between the initial two-year phase and years three through five. During the first two years, tourism, remittances, and, to a lesser extent, economic aid and export credits account for almost all of the increase, more than $1.5 billion in the first year alone. Then, in years three through five, these components, except for tourism, level off or decline somewhat, while strong growth shifts to private-sector-driven components such as assembly industry, nontraditional agriculture, mining, and foreign direct investment.

The sugar component is projected to grow only moderately, and its share of total foreign exchange receipts drops from 27 percent in the first year to only 16 percent in year five. This low and declining figure compares with 67 percent as recently as 1989, based on Soviet sugar purchases above world prices, and marks the end of two centuries of Cuban history during which sugar was king.

The Components of Foreign Exchange Receipts

A more detailed understanding of the plausibility and significance of the projection requires a closer look at each component.

Exports of Goods

Sugar. Sugar exports are projected to grow moderately from $1.2 billion to $1.5 billion over the five-year period, which, at the 1992 price of 9 cents per pound, translates to an increase from 6.3 to 7.6 million tons. Some of this increase will be in sugar-derived products such as high-sucrose syrups and packaged refined sugar. The projection is based on the assumption that there will be no substantial change in U.S. sugar import policy. U.S. sugar import quotas on a global basis totaled 1.4 million tons in 1992 and are scheduled to drop to 1.2 million tons in 1993. Even if Cuba were allotted 100 or 200 thousand tons at the expense of other countries, which would involve great difficulties for U.S. trade policy, this would only amount to 2 percent to 3 percent of Cuban sugar exports. It is also assumed that privatization of sugar lands will be a lengthier and more complicated process than in some other sectors, which could delay new investment to make sugar refineries less energy intensive and thus profitable at world prices of 10 cents or less per pound. The adoption of more stringent environmental controls could also hold back growth of production. This projection might be considered a conservative estimate, and a more ambitious alternative is discussed in the concluding section of this chapter on possible Cuban membership in NAFTA. Each additional million tons of sugar exports, however, would bring in less than $200 million of revenues, and thus sugar, even in the best of circumstances, will play a relatively small and declining role in Cuban export growth performance.

Other agriculture. The base level of $330 million of agricultural exports other than sugar is an estimate based on 1991 export levels of citrus, coffee, and tobacco of $250 million and

1989 levels (the most recent available year) for various other products. These exports are projected to grow 10 percent the first year and about 20 percent per year thereafter. Access to the U.S. market should quickly attract financing for fertilizer, new plantings, and export marketing. A trained agricultural work force and high-quality arable land are abundantly available. A quick and sharp rise in citrus export revenues, which were $120 million in 1991, can be anticipated. Current exports are of lowest-grade citrus for concentrate, a highly competitive market dominated by Brazil. With one season's application of appropriate pesticides, however, Cuban citrus can be upgraded to juice or fresh fruit quality for the U.S. market. Other likely export growth products would include mangoes, melons, pineapples, and tomatoes.

Fish. Fish exports are projected to grow from $130 million in the first year to $220 million in year five. Cuban exports were almost at the $150 million level in 1987 and 1988 but then declined to an estimated $120 million in 1992 when gasoline shortages shut down some motorized vessels. The projection here is considered reasonable if not conservative with access to the U.S. market, particularly if substantial investment in fish farming is forthcoming.

Nickel. Nickel exports are projected to rise from $300 million in year one to $500 million in year five. Based on the 1992 world price, this translates into an increase from 42,000 tons to 70,000 tons. This can be achieved by upgrades of the three existing facilities and completion of construction on the new facility at Las Camoriocas for at least partial utilization (projected full utilization is 30,000 tons). Cuba has huge reserves of nickel ore that could attract large additional foreign investments. Questions, however, about energy cost for refining the relatively low-quality Cuban ore, tightened pollution standards, and property rights for the mining sector make it unlikely that new production for export from such large new investments would come on stream during the five-year period. Foreign exchange inflow from such larger investments would fall within the foreign direct investment component, below.

Other mining. The $10 million level in year one reflects the limited exports of copper and chrome recorded in 1989. Cuba has substantial resources in these and other minerals, including manganese, laterite, and gold. Foreign mining companies are interested in developing these mineral resources but have hesitated because of the political uncertainty of mining rights obtained from the Castro government and the closed U.S. market. The projection of an increase in exports of other minerals to $150 million by year five is low compared with the longer-term potential, reflecting again the likely slower and more complicated process for establishing new mining operations.

Manufactures (mostly assembly industry). This category is projected to increase dramatically from $100 million in the first year to $900 million in year five, or by $800 million. The principal vehicle for this growth would be assembly industry within free trade zones producing textiles, footwear, electronics, sporting goods, toys, auto parts, and various other products. The projection is based on the extraordinary experience of the Caribbean regional economy during the 1980s and especially during the second half of the decade. With respect to the three-country composite, the Dominican Republic, with two-thirds the population of Cuba, increased its manufactured exports to OECD countries by $932 million from 1985 to 1990; Costa Rica and Jamaica, whose population together is only half that of Cuba, increased such exports by $431 million and $233 million respectively. Mexico increased manufactured exports, mostly from assembly industry, from $9 billion in 1985 to $22 billion in 1990, which indicates the full scope of the regional market. For each of these countries, 86 percent to 94 percent of the export growth went to the United States.

This rapid expansion of manufactured exports in the second half of the 1980s can be attributed to the earlier learning experience of both the private sector and government policymakers, which a Cuban government can adopt at the initial stage of restructuring. Private companies can now organize and build free trade zone facilities quickly, while at the same time recruiting assembly industry to occupy them. This means that hard currency begins flowing in from the outset of construction and the hiring of workers and that export shipments can begin within a year of ground breaking. Free trade zone enterprises can and should be financed by private investors with no foreign economic aid involved. The requisite host-government policy actions include making land available for free trade zones, placing priority on finance for telecommunications, container ports, and air freight infrastructure, and adopting supportive economic policies such as a convertible exchange rate and reasonable tax treatment.

The projected rapid growth of manufactured exports in a restructured Cuba would likewise require early government actions. The Castro government has already adopted laws to establish free trade zones and to attract assembly industry, although little will happen as long as the U.S. market remains closed. These laws would have to be broadened to permit private ownership in the construction and operation of the facilities. In addition, early agreements between the Cuban and U.S. governments on CBI eligibility for Cuba and access to the Overseas Private Investment Corporation for political risk insurance would give further stimulus to assembly industry.

Free trade zones of efficient scale require a land tract of about 1 million square feet, a local labor pool to provide 10,000 direct and another 10,000 to 20,000 indirect jobs, and a location within 15 miles of a container port and 30 miles of an international airport. There would likely be several such zones in the Havana region, drawing on the population concentration and the transportation infrastructure of the city. Others could be located on the northern coast, closest to the U.S. market, while the heavily populated Santiago region in the south would also lend itself to one or two zones. Yet another attractive location is Guantanamo Bay, close to nickel and tobacco production, which will lose its strategic justification to the United States as a military base once a friendly, democratic government is established in Havana. Location of free trade zones in agricultural areas, drawing on underutilized sugar land and workers, might attract, in addition to manufacturing industry, food processing industry for nontraditional farm crops.

An early infrastructure decision of broader potential for the Cuban economy would be the selection of one port, probably on the northern coast, not only as a shipping point for assembly industry and other Cuban exports but also as the Caribbean transshipment hub for regional container traffic, similar to facilities in Hong Kong and Singapore for the East Asian market. Cuba is favorably located for such a role, and existing transshipment facilities in the Dominican Republic, Puerto Rico, and Jamaica have significant drawbacks. A state-of-the-art modern container port in Cuba could be constructed and operated with the participation of private shipping companies and financed in large part by the World Bank.

Other exports. The "other export" category is a residual that was $90 million in 1992. It apparently includes some food products as well as mining and manufactured products not included in the earlier figures. This category is projected to grow about 10 percent to 20 percent per year to $200 million in the fifth year, which can be considered reasonable in view of the strong export performance projected elsewhere. In any event, this is a relatively small component of the overall projection.

Services

Hotel visitors. This is the highest growth component of all, rising from $350 million at the 1992 base level to $1.6 billion in year five of the projection, passing by sugar in the process to become the largest sector in terms of gross foreign exchange revenues. The projection during the initial two-year period is based principally on a sharp rise in the occupancy rates of existing "commercially competitive" hotel rooms and on higher average room rates as U.S. visitors predominate over European and other budget tour visitors. A strong surge of visiting businesspersons, government officials, international civil servants, Cuban Americans, and other U.S. tourists can be expected, similar to what happened in Eastern Europe but even stronger in view of the Cuban-American dimension. An increase in average occupancy for existing hotels from 55 percent to 90 percent together with a rise in average expenditure from $500 to $700 per visitor would alone raise the $350 million base figure to about $800 million. In addition, several thousand rooms not now commercially competitive could be upgraded within several months to a year, not to mention the countless smaller hostels and bed-and-breakfast facilities that would sprout forth once dollar-wielding U.S. visitors began to arrive.

To accomplish such growth, the transitional Cuban government would have to give priority to facilitating hotel renovation and support service industries from car rental and tour bus companies to restaurants and sports facilities. Privatization of hotels could move quickly because the process of hotel management by foreign companies has already begun under the Castro government. Strong growth is projected to continue in years three to five as renovation of existing hotels and construction of new hotels gather momentum. This projection also takes account of the higher than average growth of the Caribbean tourism market, compared with national income levels, over a five-year period. The $1.6 billion level of revenues in year five, based on an average per visitor expenditure of $800 in the later years, implies approximately 2 million visitors per year, or a fourfold increase over the reported level for 1992 when the U.S. embargo was still in place. This compares with 11.5 million hotel visitors to Caribbean island economies in 1990. The projection for Cuba may appear optimistic, but it is certainly feasible, especially if the Cuban government gives priority to supporting infrastructure for tourism, as explained below.

Cruise ships. All Caribbean cruise lines are anxiously awaiting the opening of Cuba for U.S. passengers and will make rapid adjustments in their schedules when this occurs. Many if not most cruises will include one day in Havana or Varadero Beach, which, for popular four-day three-night cruises in particular, will entail substantial rerouting away from the Bahamas and other more eastward islands. The initial constraint will be the lack of adequate docking and anchorage facilities. Cruise lines are optimistic, however, that interim accommodations will be devised pending the construction of permanent modern facilities. Some cruise ships will likely dock or anchor overnight in Cuba as a form of floating hotel. For the later years of the projection, improved facilities for cruise ships will permit further rapid growth. One study projects more than 1.5 million cruise passenger visits by year five, and the figure could be higher depending on available dock facilities.[1] These projections also reflect five-year growth in Caribbean cruise passengers far above the growth in national income levels.

Revenues from cruise line passengers will nevertheless be relatively small. Cruise passenger spending will likely be in the order of $50 to $100 per day, with port fees and expenditures by crew members providing some additional revenue. Based on these assumptions, foreign exchange receipts from cruise ships will rise from $50 million in year one to $150 million in year five. This projection does not include, however, the most innovative concept being considered by cruise lines, namely, direct flights from New York or Chicago to Havana, with one or two nights in a Havana hotel followed by a Caribbean cruise. This would be an attractive vacation package, with considerable additional revenues accruing to Havana hotels.

The annual arrival of 1 million to 2 million hotel guests and a similar number of cruise ship visitors, not to mention anticipated daily high-speed auto ferries from Miami and perhaps the western coast of Florida, will place enormous pressures on infrastructure for the tourism sector. Airports, docking facilities for cruise ships and auto ferries, telecommunications for hotel bookings, and ground transportation all need to be part of a broad strategy. For example, the drive by automobile from Havana to Varadero Beach now takes only an hour because there are few cars and little available gasoline. This will all change when tourists start flooding in and more Cubans are able to drive their own cars. The 60-mile Mariel-Havana-Matanzas-Varadero corridor will require an integrated grid of harbors, airports, and ground transportation infrastructure, perhaps including high-speed trains or other advanced transportation technology.

Residential construction for nonresidents. Relatively few Cuban Americans plan to return to Cuba permanently and resume Cuban citizenship, but almost all talk of vacation or retirement homes there. Many non–Cuban Americans will also see a restructured, democratic Cuba as an alternative to Mexico or Costa Rica as a place to retire. In fact, Cuba should become an extension of the two-decade building boom down both coasts of Florida in condominium and warm-weather residences for vacation, retirement, or both. Anticipated direct flights to Havana from major U.S. cities and daily auto ferries will facilitate access to a Cuba uniquely offering extended beaches and the urban charms of Havana. High-rise condominiums in Havana and Varadero Beach would likely come first. Later, the techniques of Florida developers, who obtain a large tract of waterfront property and build first a golf course and marina and then a planned community of homes, could proliferate along the hundreds of miles of Cuban coastline.

A boom in residential construction for nonresidents will undoubtedly become a major source of foreign exchange inflow as foreign purchasers finance such new construction. One thousand residences at an average price of $100,000 would bring in $100 million. The projection is for a modest level of $50 million in year two followed by a sharp rise to $500 million in year five, implying 5,000 units in the latter year. This is, of course, a best guess about an entirely new phenomenon for Cuba, but a plausible one, which perhaps will prove to be conservative.

Other services. During the 1980s, global trade in services grew faster than trade in goods—7.5 percent versus 5.5 percent annually—and developing countries have been large beneficiaries. The principal sectors for foreign exchange earnings from services for developing countries have been tourism, transportation, financial services, and wide-ranging information technology activities. There are no comprehensive statistics on trade in services by sector and country, but the Caribbean region has been a region of strong growth, integrated as it is with the highly service-oriented North American economy. A landmark "teleport" project in Kingston, Jamaica has created substantial employment of Jamaicans to supply information technology and other service-based work to the United States via satellite.

Cuba will inevitably benefit from such exports of services. With an educated labor force working for relatively low wages, Cuba could become a regional center for transportation, telecommunications, and financial services. With newly installed business infrastructure, Havana could offer clear advantages over Miami, Mexico City, and Caracas as the location for regional corporate headquarters: central location, low cost, less congestion and pollution, and a higher quality of life.

The projection for foreign exchange receipts from other services—from $50 million in year one to $250 million in year five—is a rough estimate meant to indicate a low base level and rapid growth. It could well be a conservative estimate as the North American economy becomes increasingly service-based and Cuba becomes more deeply integrated with it.

Foreign Direct Investment

The projection of actual disbursement from new foreign direct investment, from $100 million in year one up to $800 million in year five, depends heavily on the establishment of a legal framework that encourages such investment. The laws adopted by the Castro government through 1992 move in the right direction, but more definitive and far-reaching actions would be necessary, with clearly established private property rights as the starting point. This could be undertaken during the initial two-year phase for many sectors, including hotels, small- to medium-scale service and manufacturing industry, construction, and much of agriculture. Some large-scale industry and agriculture, including sugar, mining, and petroleum, could take longer to adapt to large new private investment, as reflected in the relatively low level of investment projected during the initial two to three years.

The projected levels are based on two factors. The first is a comparison with the three-country composite, where foreign direct investment in 1989-1990 was running at an annual level of $300 million to $400 million and where the investment climate, with some exceptions, was not particularly positive. The second factor is the well-known eagerness of Cuban-American businesspersons, Cuban expatriates elsewhere, and U.S. companies in general to invest in Cuba as soon as it opens. Franchises for many U.S. brand name products and services have already been committed or are under discussion with Cuban Americans and other business interests.

Remittances

The 1.1 million Cuban Americans and a substantial number of Cuban expatriates elsewhere will account for a large initial surge of foreign exchange into a restructured Cuban economy through remittances. Much of this will come in conjunction with visits to relatives to help upgrade homes, buy appliances, and improve personal consumption generally. There will likely be some additional outflow of Cubans to the United States in the first years of an open relationship, and these recent arrivals are likely to be especially generous in sending part of their earnings back to Cuba.

The $800 million level of remittances for years one and two are based, in part, on remittances by expatriates from the three-country composite, especially Dominicans and Jamaicans. Fewer than one million of those expatriates remitted $645 million in 1989 and $522 million in 1990. The substantially larger number of Cuban Americans, with a higher average income, will initially wish to do something extra after more than three decades of Cuban isolation. The $800 million projection, tapering off to $700 million in the later years, could turn out to be conservative.

Economic Assistance

Economic aid will come from bilateral donors, principally the United States, the World Bank, the InterAmerican Development Bank, and, to a much smaller extent, the UN technical agencies. It is important that the aid be used in ways that directly support the other private-sector-driven components of the projection. A recommended aid strategy to this end is elaborated in the appendix. Essentially, it rejects balance-of-payments support or other so-called cash transfers and is directed toward technical assistance, project loans for economic infrastructure and environmental cleanup, social sector support, and financial intermediaries for the private sector.

The projected level of aid begins at a low level of $100 million in year one, reflecting the slower disbursement time frame of project assistance, and builds to $800 million in year four. A decline to $700 million in year five is an indication that once private-sector-driven growth firmly takes hold, the level of official economic assistance can begin to decline. The $800 million maximum level in year four is based largely on aid levels to the three-country composite—$868 million in 1989 and $805 million in 1990. The approximate projected breakdown of the $800 million level would be multilateral development banks $300 million, the United States $300 million, other bilateral donors $150 million, and UN agencies $50 million.

Official Export Credits

Trade credits from official export credit agencies (the Export-Import Bank and the Commodity Credit Corporation for the United States) would be contingent on some understanding about outstanding official debt contracted by the Castro government, particularly the $8 billion of debt to non-U.S. Western creditors. Early agreement on an initial period of moratorium for prior debt would be reasonable, enabling new trade credits to the transitional government. Later negotiation of the old debt could presumably be kept separate from the servicing of export credits provided after the initial point of democratic transition and economic restructuring.

The projected $300 million level in year one, rising to $500 million annually in later years, is reasonable considering the overall anticipated foreign exchange earnings of the restructured economy, and it could reach somewhat higher levels. Most of it would come from the export credit agencies of the United States and other industrialized countries and from Cuba's Latin American trading partners. In addition, a special objective for a transitional Cuban government could be medium-term, three- to five-year credits for oil imports from Venezuela and Mexico. Such credits would be more advantageous than those of the San José Accord available to smaller Caribbean and Central American governments, which require 80 percent up-front cash payment. They could be justified for Cuba, at least during the first two years or so, as an extraordinary one-time action after three decades of grossly distorted trade with the Soviet bloc. Venezuela may be more disposed than Mexico to do this because it has surplus oil capacity and closer ties with Cuba in the petroleum sector, including potential collaboration in Cuba for oil refining and petrochemical production.

The Macroeconomic Outlook

The five-year projection is highly feasible, given the conditions of economic reform indicated and a reasonably positive political setting. Extrapolating this projected performance for foreign exchange receipts into a macroeconomic model for economic growth and employment is not possible in quantitative terms, however, because basic data on the Cuban economy are not available. It is not even possible to convert foreign exchange receipts into a firm figure for additional imports of capital equipment for investment and consumer goods because the foreign exchange receipts projection is in terms of gross receipts, while most of the projected components have an import content that will rise along with export receipts and data on this import feedback are also not available. Nevertheless, some clear lines of direction for the overall economy are evident.

With respect to the import content of exports, a restructured Cuba would have two distinct advantages compared with the circumstances currently facing the Castro government. The first advantage is that the degree of domestic value added should rise over time as the national economy becomes more market-oriented and competitive. A larger supply of hotel requirements, from food to furniture to air conditioners, will be supplied locally rather than imported. Sugar and nickel production will become more fuel efficient, and thus less dependent on imported petroleum, as refineries are upgraded with more modern equipment. Assembly industry, over time, tends to increase the share of local content as management is strengthened and capital equipment is added.

The second advantage is that the principal components for initial growth in foreign exchange have the highest net inflow content. Remittances, the largest growth component during the first two years, is 100 percent dollar inflow with no offsetting import content. Economic assistance likewise has a very high net inflow of hard currency because it takes the form of grants or concessionary loans with grace periods and long-term repayment schedules. Official export credits will also have a relatively high net inflow, at least during the initial years of restructuring, because there would be no offsetting repayments on earlier credits. In sum, the net inflow of foreign exchange compared with the existing situation is favorable to a restructured Cuba and should improve over time. Put another way, the projected doubling of foreign exchange receipts during the first two years should far more than double the foreign exchange available for new investment projects and consumer goods.

In any event, the export-oriented growth model presented in the CR plus five projection would generate high employment. Almost all of the key sectors projected for strong growth—tourism, other services, assembly industry, nontraditional agriculture, residential construction for nonresidents—are labor intensive and include a relatively high share of professional and high- or semi-skilled jobs. These lead sectors, moreover, will stimulate high employment growth elsewhere in the economy. A construction boom will likely sweep the country for commercial as well as residential building, involving both new construction and restoration of existing structures. Each assembly industry job creates one to two support services jobs in retail trade, commuter transportation, and residential construction. Well-paying jobs in the export-oriented sectors will, in general, stimulate all manner of consumer goods production in the national economy.

Translation of this export-led, high employment generating model into a growth rate for gross domestic product (GDP) is even more elusive, but again the rate of growth should be relatively high, probably reaching at least 5 percent annually and possibly higher by the end of the five-year period if the policy program for private-sector restructuring is forcefully implemented. Even more important than the specific rate of growth is that high growth should be sustainable over time. The five-year projection only brings the restructuring process to the point where the private-sector-driven sectors are becoming dominant, and they are the ones that can provide a self-sustaining rate of economic growth over the longer term.

Finally, there are the related issues of exchange rate for the peso, inflation, and wage levels. No projected exchange rate is attempted here, but one critical contingency will almost certainly not occur with regard to the peso, namely, uncontrolled depreciation as happened to the Russian ruble. In this most important further invidious comparison with the former Soviet Union, the key difference is the absence of an export strategy on the part of the former Soviet republics, which has led to the free fall of the ruble far below a reasonable equilibrium rate, with hugely distorting consequences for their national economies. Cuba, in contrast, will benefit from a large initial surge in foreign exchange inflow, doubling in the first two years, and this should provide confidence in the foreign exchange availability to maintain the peso in a relatively stable range of equilibrium.

Controlling the accelerating inflation currently under way in Cuba will be a matter of fiscal management. Eliminating subsidies to state enterprises and reducing the exorbitant military budget will constitute the central challenges, but the prospect of high employment growth, as explained above, should make this a less difficult process than in Europe's formerly Communist states. The Castro zero-option strategy is already undertaking a part of the adjustment by shutting down nonviable state industrial enterprises.

Wage rates in Cuba should not plunge along with the exchange rate, as is happening in Russia, but they will nevertheless remain relatively low compared with those of other countries in the Caribbean region. Although Cuban export-oriented sectors will become highly productive, wage rates tend to reflect average productivity in the national economy, and in this respect Cuba will lag badly. Overstaffing of state enterprises, a huge government bureaucracy, a military of inordinate size, and the recent shift to more primitive, labor-intensive agriculture under the zero-option strategy all drag down average productivity, and at the outset of restructuring this is where the large majority of the Cuban labor force will be located.

Thus wage rates during the initial years of a restructured Cuba will tend to be toward the low end of levels within the Caribbean region, probably less than half or only a quarter of those in Mexico and Venezuela and significantly below those in the three-country composite. Over time, if restructuring brings the positive results indicated, real wages will rise steadily. In the interim, however, relatively low wage rates in Cuba will be a mixed blessing, with the low labor and other costs making the country one of the most attractive locations in the region for new investment and job creation.

The NAFTA Option

The CR plus five projection is based on Cuba receiving MFN treatment in the U.S. market, which would include related preferential market access as a developing country. This preferential access would involve the benefits of the generalized system of tariff preferences (GSP) at the outset and negotiated qualification as a participant in the Caribbean Basin Initiative by year one or two of the transition. A more far-reaching step would be Cuban accession to the North American Free Trade Agreement. Such a step would depend on the political orientation of a democratically elected Cuban government. NAFTA membership could be resisted on the grounds that it would entail even higher dependency on the U.S. economy. On the other hand, there would be fewer deep-seated protectionist interests opposed to free trade in Cuba compared with other countries in the region because a restructured Cuba would be starting the private sector anew. In any event, if a newly democratic Cuba were to request accession to NAFTA, there would likely be a prompt and positive response by the United

States, Mexico, and Canada. This could all come about by year three or four of the five-year projection, and it is therefore appropriate to address the likely consequences here.

NAFTA is a comprehensive agreement, going far beyond the elimination of border restrictions on trade in goods. It includes open markets for trade in most services, including financial services, telecommunications, and transportation, protection of intellectual property rights, national treatment and other provisions for foreign investment, and dispute settlement mechanisms to curb unilateral restrictions, particularly by the United States. The benefits of such an agreement for the Cuban economy would fall into two distinct categories: improved access to the U.S. market and a more positive investment climate in Cuba.

Improved Cuban access to the U.S. market would be significant in a number of sectors. The textile sector could offer the greatest enhanced export prospects because U.S. tariffs as well as quotas would be eliminated under NAFTA, some immediately and others over a maximum of 10 years. It is noteworthy that U.S. tariffs on textiles and footwear are not included within the GSP and CBI preferential duty-free treatment. Cuban exports of fruits and vegetables should also benefit because most trade restrictions will be eliminated within NAFTA, although certain exceptions on sensitive trade would likely be an issue for negotiation. Exports of automotive parts from Cuba might also be stimulated significantly because NAFTA includes a provision whereby automobiles require a 62.5 percent "North American content" in order to qualify for free trade. Automotive parts sourced in Cuba would qualify as North American content, and with wage rates in Cuba far below those in Mexico, automobile companies, Japanese as well as U.S., would find it attractive to establish production in Cuba. An additional benefit for such companies would be the resulting positive corporate image in a Cuban market for motor vehicle sales growing rapidly after more than 30 years of embargo and very low imports.

Access to the U.S. market for Cuban sugar would be a major issue of negotiation for Cuban access to NAFTA, but the outcome is unpredictable and likely to provide only limited benefits to Cuba. NAFTA provides gradual liberalization of bilateral Mexico-U.S. trade in sugar, the application of tariff quotas on third-country imports after 6 years, and total elimination of restrictions on bilateral trade after 15 years. Cuban accession would nevertheless certainly entail special provisions for the very large Cuban sugar production. A modest, gradually increasing quota over a lengthy 10- to 15-year period, with a scheduled review of the situation at the end of the period, would be one possible outcome. The bold option would be a 15-year transition to free trade in sugar between the United States and Cuba, but this would mean a fundamental change in U.S. sugar policy from the current highly protected domestic price, which is more than double the world market price. Such a restructuring, with corresponding adjustment assistance for domestic sugar producers, is feasible in a U.S. political climate stressing the need to strengthen international competitiveness and could be helped by support from influential Cuban-American sugar producers in the United States if they chose to sacrifice protection in the U.S. market for new opportunities in Cuba. At this point, however, the likelihood of such an outcome appears to be very low.

The improved investment climate in Cuba from NAFTA membership could be even more beneficial to Cuban economic recovery and growth. NAFTA membership would constitute the most credible assurance that the market-oriented restructuring within Cuba would not be reversed. Provisions in the areas of trade in services, investment, and intellectual property rights would be decisive factors for many potential investors, while duty-free entry into Cuba would reduce costs for many industries and restrain inflation. All of these arguments were used by President Carlos Salinas de Gortari of Mexico and his government in making the case for Mexican membership in NAFTA, and they could apply even more forcefully for the smaller Cuban economy, which would be under a cloud of political uncertainty after so many years of Communist rule and isolation.

The aggregate economic benefits to Cuba from NAFTA membership cannot be quantified, but they would certainly raise substantially the $9.5 billion projection for foreign exchange receipts in year five as well as the economic growth path beyond. More fundamentally, Cuban entry into NAFTA would extend the integrated North American/Caribbean market a critical step forward by incorporating the centrally located and largest island in the

Caribbean. This would have, in addition to the direct effects on the Cuban economy, substantial impact on others in the region, particularly the other island republics. Indeed, the increasingly imminent prospect of a restructured Cuba with access to the U.S. market is already focusing minds in both the private and public sectors throughout the region.

6
The Impact on Others in the Region

The reintegration of Cuba will have substantial impact throughout the Caribbean regional economy, but the impact will be very uneven by sector and country. There are also important distinctions between the short-term adjustments that are likely to take place in trade and investment patterns and the longer-term restructuring of economic and political relationships.

The subject of Cuban regional economic participation, once normal commercial relations have been reestablished with the United States, is receiving growing attention elsewhere in the region, with those in the private sectors generally better informed and more forward-thinking than government officials. Businesspersons travel more frequently to Cuba than political leaders do, have extensive contact with Cuban technocrats and enterprise managers, and, of course, have direct financial interests at stake. In contrast, political leaders, although they understand the political and economic dead end facing the Castro Communist regime, generally limit their contacts to a sterile official dialogue and are preoccupied with other issues such as NAFTA, the CBI, CARICOM reform, and selling bananas to the European Community. A widespread belief in both the public and private sectors is that Castro's charismatic leadership abilities will enable him to maintain control for some years to come. This assessment is often influenced, however, by veiled admiration of Castro's long-standing defiance of the United States and by a lack of knowledge about how bleak the current economic crisis in Cuba really is.

Attitudes elsewhere in the region vary considerably by country. Mexico has had the deepest and broadest contact with Castro's Cuba over the past 30 years but at this point is among the least concerned about Cuba's future. Mexico is rightly preoccupied with its own transition to an industrialized democracy and is interested primarily in the U.S. relationship and secondarily in its relationships with Western Europe and East Asia. It is not surpris-

ing that President Salinas received Cuban exile leaders Jorge Mas
Canosa and Carlos Montaner in Mexico in August 1992 to give
them assurances of no new Mexican aid to Cuba in order to avoid
the exiles' opposition to the approval of NAFTA by the U.S.
Congress. A few Mexican economic interests would be affected by
a restructured Cuba, among them some increased competition in
the tourism sector and some new export opportunities in Cuba.
But these would be infinitesimal compared with the North
American market. The Mexican government assesses Fidel Castro
as intransigent in resisting fundamental economic reform and
democratization. One can imagine the clash in personalities
between the U.S.-trained technocrat Salinas and the bearded
Cuban revolutionary during several meetings over the past two
years. Mexican officials are concerned about instability and widespread violence during the inevitable Cuban transition and refer
to the current Panama situation as something to avoid. Aside from
that, Cuba policy basically receives a shoulder shrug.

Aside from the occasional summit dialogue with Fidel Castro,
Venezuela is also largely unconcerned with Cuba. Preoccupation
with political instability and controversial economic reforms at
home is the main reason. Two exceptions to this lack of concern,
however, stand out. The first—more keenly felt in the private sector—is apprehension that a restructured Cuba will cause significant competitive harm to the Venezuelan tourism sector and
fledgling but not yet very successful assembly industry, such as for
footwear production. The second exception is the petroleum sector. Over the years, Venezuela has been deeply engaged with Cuba
in a triangular relationship with the Soviet Union regarding petroleum. Venezuela shipped oil directly to Cuba while the Soviet
Union sold its own oil on the West European market and then
made payment directly to the government of Venezuela for the
Venezuelan oil that Cuba received. This triangular relationship is
now greatly reduced if not terminated, but Cuban-Venezuelan ties
between their respective energy and other interested ministries
continue to be close. With a restructured Cuba, Venezuela has
hopes of joint ventures in Cuba for oil refining and petrochemical
production for the Cuban market. As noted earlier, this interest
could be stimulated by export credits for Venezuelan oil exports to
Cuba at the outset of the transition.

Compared to Mexico and Venezuela, the Caribbean island republics will be more directly and substantially affected by the regional reintegration of Cuba, with some significant adverse effects, at least during the initial years. The most active consideration of the consequences of Cuba's reintegration is taking place in the Dominican Republic and Jamaica, primarily by the private-sector leaders. The Dominican Republic is probably more vulnerable to new Cuban competition. The Dominican tourism sector has lower-priced, economy hotels that would be more directly competitive with many Cuban hotels. European package tours to both Cuba and the Dominican Republic are currently doing well, but North American tourists may choose Cuba instead of the Dominican Republic. Burgeoning assembly industry since the late 1980s has been a major stimulus to a Dominican economy otherwise troubled by fiscal mismanagement and overregulation, and free zone development in Cuba could offer an attractive alternative to the Dominican Republic. Dominican agriculture would also face direct Cuban competition ranging from sugar to citrus to other fruits and vegetables, and representatives of Dominican agribusinesses have been visiting Cuba with a view to joint ventures for upgrading existing Cuban citrus production and planting new pineapple acreage and citrus trees. The broadest concern of the Dominican private sector is that a very positive investment climate could develop in Cuba, diverting potential investors from the Dominican Republic in many sectors.

The Jamaican business community is even more engaged than the Dominican in assessing its interests in a restructured Cuba, and many heads of companies have recently made trips there. The assessment in Jamaica, moreover, is, on balance, more positive about potential opportunities in a reopened Cuba. Direct investment or joint ventures in Cuba are being pursued or considered for hotels, citrus and other agricultural products, financial services, and some industry sectors. Jamaican entrepreneurial talent and marketing experience in Europe as well as in the United States are viewed as a good fit for alliances with Cuban low-cost human and natural resources. Even for tourism, complementarity is seen between Cuban facilities and higher-quality Jamaican resorts through package tours to both countries, which are already happening. Nevertheless, for Jamaican hotels, and, even more so, for a struggling Jamaican assembly industry, the growing likelihood of a dynamic new Cuba, four times the size of Jamaica and located between Jamaica and the essential U.S. market, is a troubling prospect.

The smaller Caribbean countries are concerned about a reintegrated Cuba for the same reasons that the larger island republics are, and in some cases more so and for good reason. Tourism is often the number one hard currency earner, and a reopened Cuba could draw away many hotel guests and cruise ships. Investment climate in the smaller islands is more fragile, domestic industry higher-cost, and the political outlook frequently more clouded. There is already deep concern that NAFTA will divert new investment away from the Caribbean islands to Mexico. The possibility that Cuba would seek early membership in NAFTA as well is a mind-boggling thought. The incisive one-liner bandied about is that the only thing the small Caribbean island economies fear more than a Communist Cuba is a competitive, market-oriented Cuba.

Other participants in the Caribbean regional economy that will be affected by a restructured Cuba include Central America, Colombia, Haiti, the Bahamas, and Puerto Rico, not to mention Florida and other coastal zones of the United States. Each has distinctive characteristics that will bear on the outcome, and all would benefit from a closer analysis than was possible during the course of this study.

The principal conclusion from all of the foregoing is the need for a more coherent regional analytic framework for the anticipated reintegration of Cuba. Such a framework does not currently exist, however, partly for institutional reasons and partly from a policy orientation that still emphasizes cold war alignments. The World Bank and the InterAmerican Development Bank, for example, would be logical institutions in which to examine the regional economic implications of a restructured Cuba, but their professional staffs are precluded from doing so because Cuba is not a member of the banks.

Analysis within the U.S. government is less inhibited by the lack of formal diplomatic relations with Cuba, but policy research units in the State Department and elsewhere in the executive branch still tend to separate Cuba from other Caribbean countries, which makes integrated analysis on a regional basis difficult. The organization of the State Department's Bureau of Inter-American Affairs is the most glaring example of a disintegrated approach to the Caribbean region. Below the assistant secretary level, one deputy assistant secretary has responsibility for Cuba, a second for Mexico and other Caribbean countries, a third for Central America, and a fourth for Venezuela and Colombia as primarily parts of South America. Political and economic realities are gathering momentum toward ever deeper Caribbean Basin regional integration, while the bureau's organizational chart effectively precludes policy formulation in such regional terms.

A more coherent analytic framework for Cuban reintegration into the Caribbean region would have to address three interrelated dimensions, two essentially economic in character and the third pertaining to government policy. The first dimension concerns the short-term market reactions to a restructured Cuba and a lifting of the U.S. embargo. Shifts in trade and investment patterns would reflect a revised set of comparative advantages within the region as augmented by Cuban participation. The second dimension would be the longer-term impact of higher overall growth and a more fundamental geographic restructuring of the regional economy. These two economic dimensions are akin to the traditional short-term "static" and longer-term "dynamic" effects of formation of a customs union or a free trade area. The third, policy dimension can be summed up as what happens next in the region after NAFTA is implemented. The following are some preliminary thoughts on each of the three dimensions.

Short-term Shifts in Trade and Investment

Some specifics of short-term adjustment to a reopened Cuba have already been described for neighboring countries. The principal sectors involved coincide with the orientation of the new Caribbean economic order: tourism, other services, nontraditional agriculture, and assembly industry. The dynamics of trade adjustment will likely vary substantially among specific product categories. Export patterns for rum, cigars, paintings, and artifacts will all change to incorporate new Cuban participation. For broader sectors, such as textiles and electronics, corporate strategies by East Asian and European as well as U.S. companies will factor in the possibility of Cuban production as part of the sourcing in the Caribbean region. Many companies are already planning for such an adjustment, but U.S. companies, in particular, are doing so in a very quiet way so as to avoid the appearance of wanting to deal with the Castro government.

The key question is whether exports by or investment in Cuba will be "trade-creating" or "trade-diverting," to adopt again the traditional terminology for the creation of a customs union. Trade-creating means that new Cuban exports would be additional to existing exports by others in the region and thus result in an overall increase in trade. Trade-diverting, in contrast, would mean that Cuban exports would displace existing exports by others. A similar distinction can be made for investment in Cuba.

The trade-creation versus trade-diversion effects cannot be predicted with any precision, but they will probably vary substantially among the key sectors affected. Tourism holds the greatest prospect for a trade-creating effect, although there will be some trade diversion as well. Many tourists, businesspersons, and officials who will visit a reopened Cuba will be additions to the existing Caribbean visitor inflow. Curiosity to see a revived Havana will draw visitors who would not otherwise come to the Caribbean. Many Cuban Americans and other expatriate Cubans would clearly be additional travelers. Other island resorts could experience a net benefit as new visitors stop over in conjunction with a visit to Cuba. Cruise ship visitors to Cuba would likely be more trade-diverting, at least during the first few years, because the limiting constraint on regional travel is the number of available cruise ships.1 Overall, however, Caribbean tourism should benefit from a significant trade-creating effect, even in the short run, and the higher than average growth rates in the region should rise even higher.

The outlook for nontraditional agricultural exports to the U.S. market is less clear. New Cuban exports of citrus and other fruits and vegetables could be additional to existing Caribbean exports, but there are quantitative limits on U.S. imports, often of a seasonal nature, based on closely administered marketing regulations. This could put new Cuban exports in trade-diverting competition with others in the region. To the extent that NAFTA provides Mexico with preferred access to the U.S. market, the marketing regulations could intensify Cuban competition with other island republics and Central America.

The burgeoning assembly industry operations in the Caribbean region, for export to the U.S. market, are more likely to tend toward trade-diverting results. Corporate decisions often involve establishing a new facility for particular operations in the Caribbean region, for which a cross-country survey is taken of various cost and other factors for deciding where the facility will be located. With Cuba accessible, a decision to locate there would be at the expense of location elsewhere in the region. There is also the likelihood of a trade-diverting effect on existing Caribbean assembly facilities. Such facilities can be shifted quickly and relatively cheaply from one country to another if significant cost and other advantages materialize, which could be the case with a reopened Cuba. The broad outlook for assembly industry in the region, however, has to take account of the overall rapid growth that will likely continue. In this context, the trade-diverting effects of a reintegrated Cuba could, in some instances, result in a lower rate of growth rather than in an absolute decline elsewhere in the region.

More precise estimates of the short-term trade-creating and trade-diverting effects caused by a reintegrated Cuba would require surveys of corporate intent for key sectors. This is a normal practice for assessing basic changes in trade and investment relationships, as was done, for example, in anticipating both the impact of the EC 92 program of market unification and NAFTA. It would be appropriate at this time to undertake similar survey work for a Cuba reintegrated within the Caribbean region.

Longer-term Growth and Restructuring

A reintegrated Cuba, over the longer term, should stimulate a higher rate of overall regional economic growth and lead to fundamental changes in the structure of the Caribbean regional economy. To draw, one more time, on the analogy with the short-term static and longer-term dynamic effects of customs union formation, the longer-term dynamic effects are more likely to be positive but, at the same time, more elusive to specify or quantify. As a result, greater attention tends to be given to the short-term impact, including adverse effects on outsiders, which can be quantified, and less to the more amorphous yet positive longer-term gains.

The central argument for a longer-term positive effect on the region from Cuban reintegration is that growth in trade and investment within Cuba will have a stimulative spinoff elsewhere in the region. Direct trade between Cuba and its neighboring countries and joint production or marketing arrangements will tend to increase trade and production throughout the region. The demonstration effect of an open, high-growth Cuban economy should also influence the political leadership elsewhere to emulate the Cuban model and thereby stimulate further regional growth in trade and investment.

In addition to this general line of argumentation for higher economic growth, a number of more specific changes in the structure of the regional economy caused by Cuban reintegration will also likely have a positive impact on neighboring countries. One such structural change will be a reorientation of economic infrastructure, particularly in the transportation and communications sectors. Air and sea transportation networks will shift to make Cuba the natural geographic hub it once was. Aside from the direct gains to Cuba, this should draw the other island economies closer together into a more integrated subregion. A similar effect would be likely to the extent that international telecommunications and related financial services, as well as regional corporate headquarters, tend to locate in Havana.

Another longer-term effect, building on the more integrated infrastructure, would be for companies to view the Caribbean island economies as a far more substantial regional market of some 30 million people, worthy of greater attention. Two-way trade and a corporate presence in the market through investment should grow accordingly, which would, in turn, have a self-reinforcing impact on economic growth and the investment climate.

Yet another longer-term effect of more profound consequence would be the progressive merging of the economies of Cuba and southern Florida. Cuba, to a growing extent, would be an extension of the southeastern peninsula of the United States in economic terms, a connection solidified by the interaction of the Cuban populations on either side of the straits of Florida. In effect, an economic and cultural bridge would be built from southern

Florida to the center of the Caribbean island economy, drawing
neighboring islands more closely into the process at the same
time.

Finally, the emergence of Cuba as an active, substantial participant at the center of the Caribbean economy will alter the balance of political relationships in the region. With implementation
of NAFTA, the legitimate concern of Caribbean island economies
is that the U.S.-Mexico relationship will become overwhelming,
with Central American countries becoming increasingly an
appendage to the U.S.-Mexico bloc. The reentry of Cuba into the
regional balance, however, could establish a greatly enhanced
counterweight grouping, drawing together Cuba with the
Dominican Republic, the CARICOM countries, and perhaps
Venezuela. Such a development is more contingent than the other
longer-term directions of change on the policy relationship that
will evolve between the United States and a reopened Cuba, a relationship that will be of considerable importance for all others in
the region.

What Next after NAFTA?

A major question of trade strategy for the new Clinton administration will be whether and in what directions to pursue comprehensive free trade agreements patterned on NAFTA. The Bush administration envisaged NAFTA as the first step to free trade
throughout the Western Hemisphere and toward the end of its
tenure proposed selective free trade agreements with East Asian
and East European countries as well. The next in line for free
trade after NAFTA is Chile, whose free trade approach would
make negotiation of such an agreement relatively simple. The
dynamic unleashed by NAFTA, however, is having more concentrated impact on the smaller Caribbean Basin economies, whose
trade dependencies with North America are far higher than those
of South American countries. The policy question of what next
after NAFTA has most pressing significance for these Caribbean
economies as regional economic integration progressively widens
and deepens. This momentum for regional broadening of NAFTA
to neighboring countries in the Caribbean Basin can be referred
to as the spreading inkblot effect.

The day after the U.S. embargo on Cuba is lifted, post-NAFTA trade strategy for the Caribbean region will have to include Cuba, with wide-ranging consequences. A U.S.-CARICOM free trade agreement, for example, would become peripheral, and preliminary discussion about free trade with Venezuela, Costa Rica, or other countries in the region could be influenced greatly by the course of the U.S.-Cuban relationship. These various potential post-NAFTA negotiations, moreover, may merge into the same time frame. President Clinton is unlikely to obtain congressional authority to negotiate further free trade agreements before 1994, and formal negotiations, even with Chile, could extend into 1995. By that time, Cuba could well be launched onto the market-oriented restructuring described in this study. Policy planning for the Caribbean region can no longer exclude the contingency of full Cuban participation.

It is still far from clear whether any other countries in the Caribbean region will, in fact, be prepared to enter into the comprehensive free trade commitments contained in NAFTA. Costa Rica, Venezuela, and Jamaica are more advanced in policy reform toward free trade than others, but the fundamental political commitment of fully opening their smaller economies to the North American market has not yet been faced. The future course of Cuba is even less clear and, indeed, is highly speculative at this point. Nevertheless, a negotiated entry of Cuba into NAFTA over the next several years is a distinct possibility. A transition period of 10 years or more could ease the adjustment of the Cuban economy, which in any event would be building anew in its private-sector orientation.

Even preliminary U.S.-Cuban talks about a free trade agreement would force others to reassess their trade strategies. The Dominican Republic and Jamaica would face the choice of following suit or being left outside, at serious competitive disadvantage. The smaller CARICOM countries, in any event physically distant from Jamaica, would have difficulty maintaining the attention of the grouping's predominant member. Venezuela, Colombia, and the Central American republics would also have to focus more urgently on whether they can afford to remain apart from an inclusive North American free trade arrangement that is spreading to the larger and closer Caribbean island republics.

This may all appear an exercise in extravagant speculation, but only four years ago the idea of U.S.-Mexican free trade was generally considered fatuous, and the collapse of the Soviet Union was not addressed seriously by anyone. The Caribbean regional economy is in a state of flux with the advent of NAFTA, and some major further steps toward integration will surely occur during the course of the 1990s. Within this time frame, a restructured and reintegrated Cuba will likely be a, if not the, principal force for creating the post-NAFTA Caribbean economic order.

7
The U.S. Policy Response

Circumstances have changed fundamentally within Cuba from the abrupt cutoff of Soviet aid, within the Caribbean region from restructured trade and investment patterns, and within a post–cold war global order in the broadest terms. Together, these changes more than warrant a fresh and forward-looking policy reassessment of the U.S.-Cuba relationship by the new Clinton administration in Washington and, it is to be hoped, by the Castro government in Havana as well.

The economic analysis in this study produces three principal conclusions that should form the point of departure for such a reassessment:

- The cutoff of Soviet aid has led to a 73 percent decline in Cuban imports, including an estimated 86 percent drop in imported machinery and equipment. As a consequence, new investment projects have ground to a halt and maintenance of the existing industrial base and economic infrastructure is neglected. A cumulative process of structural deterioration—*desmoronamiento*—is taking place and will continue until sustained economic recovery is achieved.
- The current Cuban strategy of making limited economic reforms while the U.S. embargo remains in place will produce no significant improvement over the next several years, and imports could drop even further. Progressive deterioration of the economy will continue.
- In contrast, a basic restructuring to a market-oriented economy—in conjunction with a lifting of the U.S. embargo—could produce an extraordinarily rapid and robust recovery, particularly because of the unique economic realities of the new Caribbean economic order. The Castro government is simply wrong in predicting economic chaos and collapse from such a restructuring.

These analytic conclusions clearly point to a policy course for

76

Cuba of market-oriented restructuring at the earliest possible time, before the Cuban economy deteriorates much further. Moreover, the restructuring will produce the projected early economic recovery only if it is accompanied by a nondisruptive and democratic political transition. Unfortunately, however, the judgment of Cuba experts tends to be pessimistic that such an early restructuring will occur. Rather, the outcome widely predicted is either very gradual—and thus ineffectual—reform within a still predominantly state-controlled economy or a prolonged period of political instability and violence.[1] The resulting consequence, in either event, would be continued stagnation and decline.

The outlook, however, need not be so bleak. Communist regimes in Eastern Europe and the former Soviet Union have opted for democratization and radical economic reform notwithstanding earlier expert opinion to the contrary. The demonstration effect of market-oriented economic success—first in East Asia and more recently in Mexico, Argentina, and other countries in the Western Hemisphere—should progressively influence beleaguered thinking within Cuba. The response of other countries to the changed circumstances facing Cuba can also play a significant role in the outcome. The U.S. policy response, most particularly, can be an important factor.

The analytic conclusions drawn from this study indeed point to the need for a revised U.S. policy toward Cuba. The central policy objective should remain the earliest possible transition of Cuba to democracy and market-oriented economic recovery. The policy response, however, should be more forceful than the largely passive policy of the Bush administration, which consisted essentially of waiting for the Castro regime to collapse from within. Although the Cuban economy under communism will continue to deteriorate, there is no clear indication of an early political crisis given the extensive security apparatus of the government, and, in any event, an ultimate confrontational showdown could produce widespread violence and prolonged political instability.

A more proactive U.S. policy is in order, one that combines positive incentives, or "carrots," for movement toward political and economic reform with disincentives, or "sticks," for continued intransigence with respect to nondemocratic government and the abuse of basic human rights. The 1992 Cuban Democracy Act embodies, in principle, such a more proactive policy course, although in final form the sticks of extended embargo far outweigh the carrots for reform. The U.S. House Foreign Affairs Committee report states that

> the purpose of H.R. 5323 [the Cuban Democracy Act of 1992] is to promote peaceful democratic change in Cuba through the application of appropriate pressures on the Cuban Government and through support for the Cuban people. . . . The bill sets forth a series of measures, consisting of both carrots and sticks, designed to hasten a democratic transition in Cuba by increasing the isolation of the regime while creating openings to democratic opposition groups that will shape Cuba's future.[2]

A Proactive Strategy

The U.S. policy response presented here constitutes an extended and more balanced proactive strategy for the same purposes as stated for the Cuban Democracy Act. It consists of three principal substantive elements and one pervading concept. The three substantive elements are broader dialogue, a more proactive bilateral agenda, and concerted multilateral diplomacy. The pervading concept is that of reconciliation.

Broadened and More Open Dialogue

The Communist regime in Cuba is at a dead end politically and economically and the need for change is broadly recognized within the country. But the direction and degree of change are viewed with uncertainty. Widespread support for the ill-defined objectives of "the Revolution" still exists, mixed with anxiety about whether the U.S. government and Cuban Americans intend to reassert some form of control over Cuban society.

This situation lends itself to a more intense and broadened dialogue between Cuba and the United States to elaborate the mutual benefits to be derived from a democratic and market-oriented transition in Cuba. The form of the dialogue should be more open than it has been in the past and should include various sectors of leadership and expertise in both countries. During the second Nixon/Ford and the Carter administrations, a highly restrictive and secret dialogue was pursued with Fidel Castro and his most senior advisers to resolve the political impasse between the two countries. The Cuban president's indisputable control at that time, with massive Soviet economic support, justified a narrowly focused dialogue with the top leadership. Now, however, the widely questioned and near hopeless prospect for a continued course of unyielding Communist political rule and rigid state control of the economy dictate a broader and more open exchange of views.

In terms of political dialogue, visits to Cuba by a wider range of knowledgeable U.S. citizens, in and out of the government, and U.S.-Cuban discussion forums outside Cuba should be encouraged to explain clearly what the United States means by support for democratization and for free and open elections. Discussion of the kinds of technical assistance offered elsewhere in the hemisphere should make clear that the United States does not intend to interfere with the sovereign choice of the Cuban people on internal matters. Nor does it intend to impede the continuance or further development of the social dimensions of the Cuban revolution, such as in the health care and education sectors. The dialogue should leave no doubt, however, that the core political problems of abuse of basic human rights and absence of political freedoms must be addressed by Cuba as part of any transition.

Many observers feel that meaningful political dialogue with Cuba is impossible as long as Fidel Castro remains the country's leader. That may well be the case. Nevertheless, holding the dialogue is in itself important, both to reestablish lines of communication that have been closed for more than 30 years and to educate and prepare future Cuban leaders to move away from Castro's intransigent positions.

The economic dialogue lends itself to even more expansive broadening in view of the current financial crisis in Cuba and the wide-ranging potential for mutual benefits once the bilateral relationship is normalized. The lines of analysis developed in this study could be elaborated and compared with counterpart economic projections being developed within Cuba. The annual meeting of the Association for the Study of the Cuban Economy, for example, could be expanded to include full participation by

Cuban economists.[3] U.S. economic expertise should not be limited to Latin America specialists but should include those with recent experience in economic transition in Eastern Europe. U.S. businessmen and women, currently prohibited from visiting Cuba, could add a broad dimension of realism and practical business judgment to the dialogue if they were permitted to visit Cuba and meet with enterprise managers, technocrats, and other professionals in their respective sectors.

An enhanced official dialogue, including both political and economic issues, would presumably lead to discussion of actions to deal with specific problems and to improve the relationship in broader terms—in other words, a more proactive bilateral agenda.

A More Proactive Bilateral Agenda

Policy actions on the part of the United States to encourage early, nonviolent transition in Cuba could take many forms and would be tailored to circumstances as they evolve in Cuba. They would consist of both carrots and sticks, but the balance between the two should tilt more heavily toward carrots, or positive incentives. In view of the growing isolation of hard-line Communist thinking within Cuba and to minimize violence when change does occur, it is appropriate for the United States to err on the side of positive steps toward reconciliation rather than a more threatening confrontation.

The "big carrot," of course, would be a lifting of the U.S. embargo on trade and travel. A full lifting of the embargo would not be advisable, however, absent a clear commitment by Cuba to an irrevocable course of democratization and economic reform. As discussed in chapter 3, a premature lifting of the embargo would bring substantial immediate financial relief to the Castro government, allowing a rigid Communist regime to continue for a considerably longer time. It would prompt a declaration of diplomatic victory by Fidel Castro that, together with inevitable growing pressures for internal reform, could increase the chances for later violent confrontation. In any event, statements by President Clinton dating back to his electoral campaign and views expressed by the U.S. Congress preclude a unilateral U.S. lifting of the embargo for the foreseeable future.

Short of this "big carrot," a number of actions could be considered as a basis for a more active bilateral agenda. Formulation of a specific agenda is not possible without detailed knowledge of developments as they evolve within Cuba. Illustrative of possible early positive incentives, however, would be eased trade restrictions for medicines and other humanitarian-related products. Some relaxation of travel restrictions has already been mentioned in relation to a broadened dialogue. Positive actions by the United States would be related to corresponding moves by the Cuban government to ease bilateral problems and improve communication between the two countries. The thorniest potential bilateral issue impeding normalization of U.S.-Cuban relations is that of expropriation claims by U.S. citizens, valued at almost $2 billion at the time of expropriation and now totaling about $5.5 billion with cumulated interest. No quick breakthrough can be expected on this issue, but work on the more technical aspects of resolving these claims, in the context of U.S. law and a wide range of precedents elsewhere, could begin at a relatively early point.

Punitive disincentives to continued human rights abuse and the absence of political freedoms could involve tightened trade sanctions and diplomatic initiatives. Such actions would be more effective, however, to the extent they were pursued on a more concerted, multilateral basis.

A Concerted Multilateral Diplomacy

U.S. Cuba policy has been overwhelmingly bilateral in character, and, in key respects, the United States is at odds with its closest allies and neighbors. The principal exception wherein a multilateral approach has been pursued is in the UN Human Rights Commission, where a majority of members supports the U.S. initiative to condemn Cuban violations of basic human rights. Even in this context, however, recently obtained supporting votes have come from members of the former Soviet bloc, in some cases now far removed from significant influence on Cuba, rather than from Cuba's neighbors in the hemisphere and its industrialized trading partners.

A strengthened and more cohesive multilateral diplomacy could be helpful in bringing about an early, nonviolent transition in Cuba. Key countries for such a multilateral diplomacy are

Mexico, Spain, and Venezuela, which have a direct dialogue with Fidel Castro and have urged on him an early democratic political transition and market-oriented economic reforms. There has been little attempt to coordinate this dialogue with U.S. Cuba policy, however, largely because the others oppose a continued U.S. embargo—a disagreement aggravated by the 1992 Cuban Democracy Act, which attempts to extend the embargo to U.S. affiliates in other countries.

U.S. Cuba policy will remain principally bilateral in content, but a closer, mutually supportive approach with others should be possible if U.S. strategy, even with the embargo still in place, were developed in a less confrontational manner. There would be common cause to bring about an early and nonviolent transition in Cuba. The United States could clarify that it is not seeking a disruptive upheaval of Cuban society. Others could bring more pointed pressure on the Castro government for early change, with consideration of at least diplomatic and perhaps other more substantive actions if the Castro government were not responsive. Such an approach would be in keeping, for example, with actions recently taken by the Organization of American States (OAS) to strengthen its support of democracy in the Western Hemisphere.

A more concerted approach by the United States and the three principal interlocutors with Cuba could be extended to other countries in the hemisphere and to Cuba's industrialized trading partners. The announcement by the United States and others of a concerted strategy to democratize Cuba, however general in content and objective, could have a positive psychological impact on attitudes toward democratic change within Cuba. In the context of more cooperative actions by others, the extension of the U.S. embargo to affiliates of U.S. companies abroad should be reconsidered in view of the political sensitivity to this extraterritorial encroachment and its exploitation by the Castro government.

One other area of multilateral initiative that could be pursued concerns the international financial institutions. Cuba is not a member of the IMF, the World Bank, or the InterAmerican Development Bank, and professional staff in these institutions are precluded from even beginning to analyze the elements of financial stabilization or economic restructuring programs for Cuba. Drawing on the precedent of the former Soviet Union, however, informal consultations between Cuban officials and professional staff of these financial institutions could begin at an early point, once the Cuban government indicates a serious intention to undertake basic political and economic reforms. This could be a useful educational step to prepare the way for the actual process of economic restructuring, and support for it by the United States would send a constructive signal to Havana.

Reconciliation: The Pervading Concept

Such initiatives on the bilateral and multilateral diplomatic fronts would constitute clear signals of a broader strategy to support early change in Cuba on the basis of reconciliation rather than confrontation. Reconciliation will be most difficult among Cubans, both within Cuba and between those in Cuba and those abroad, particularly in the United States. The United States should support such reconciliation among Cubans through the establishment of democratic government and respect for individual rights. Certainly, acts of terrorism against the Castro government should be condemned just as are repressive acts against the Cuban people by the prevailing Communist regime in Havana.

Reconciliation between the United States and Cuba will also be difficult after more than three decades of hostility and isolation. On the Cuban side, suspicion of U.S. motives dates back a century to the U.S. imposition of the Platt amendment on the first constitution of a Cuba liberated from Spain, which permitted U.S. intervention in a consequently less than fully independent Cuba. A clear U.S. renunciation of any form of future Platt amendment would be a message welcomed by the Cuban people.

Reconciliation, among Cubans and between Cuba and the United States, will ultimately take place, and the issue is how to hasten the process. The mutual interests and opportunities in building a prosperous Caribbean regional economy—with the twin poles of southern Florida and Cuba—will form the foundation. Colonialism is a spent concept. So, too, are Communist political rule and state-controlled national economies. It is time to move on to a new Caribbean economic order through the earliest and least disruptive possible transition in Cuba. The economic realities speak for themselves. The other necessary ingredient is a political leadership in both countries that looks to the future and not to the past. The inspiration can be drawn from José Martí, the revered Cuban poet and leader of Cuba's war for independence:

¡*Cultivemos una rosa blanca!*
Let us cultivate a white rose!

Appendix
An Economic Assistance
Strategy for Cuba

Foreign economic assistance has an important role to play in achieving Cuba's successful economic transition to an export-oriented, private-sector-driven economy. The strategy must encompass both quantitative and qualitative objectives. Projecting quantitative levels of assistance is relatively straightforward, based on aid flows to other countries in the region and the anticipated priority status Cuba will acquire during the initial years of transition. The qualitative factors—how the aid is used and what it should accomplish—are less clear yet even more crucial to the outcome.

Quantitative levels of economic assistance are contained in chapter 5's five-year projection, building up from $100 million of disbursements in the first year to a high of $800 million in year four before tapering off to $700 million in the fifth year as private-sector-driven growth becomes self-sustaining. The projected sources of finance for the $800 million maximum level are $300 million from the multilateral development banks (the World Bank and the InterAmerican Development Bank), $300 million from the United States, $150 million from other bilateral donors (West European nations, Japan, and Canada), and $50 million from specialized agencies of the United Nations (the UN Development Program, UNESCO, the World Health Organization, the UN Environmental Program, and others). These are rough yet reasonable orders of magnitude. For example, in 1989, as shown in table 1.5, the three-country composite of Costa Rica, the Dominican Republic and Jamaica received economic assistance disbursements of $870 million, of which the multilateral development banks supplied $238 million. The $300 million level of projected U.S. assistance is similarly in keeping with aid levels to priority countries in the region during active phases of transition.

It is the structure of the assistance program that will be critical, however, not only for obtaining political support for the projected quantitative levels of aid but also for achieving the central objective of support for a market-oriented transition of the Cuban economy. Experience during the 1980s, in the Caribbean region and elsewhere, is mixed as to the effectiveness of economic aid, and in some cases large amounts of official financial support have been counterproductive, slowing down the reform process through overly generous cash payments to reform-resistant governments. Economic aid, in such circumstances, can become a financial cushion to postpone unpopular economic reforms and to retain excessive economic control by the central government.[1]

The starting point for an aid strategy for Cuba is to avoid cash transfers to the central government or other forms of fast-disbursing balance-of-payments support. Instead, assistance should be targeted on the implementation of specific priority projects, as explained below. Developing countries in extreme financial crisis, which may currently include the former Soviet Union, may require some cash transfer assistance to avert economic collapse, but this should not be the case for a restructured Cuba. As shown in the Cuba Restructured Plus Five projection (table 5.1), foreign exchange receipts will quickly rise from tourism, remittances, and other sources. Economic aid consequently can be targeted more effectively on projects of direct support to the transition program, even though such project assistance is relatively slow-disbursing.

Such "projectized" economic assistance would fall into four principal categories: technical assistance, economic infrastructure, social sector support, and financial intermediaries for the private sector. The detailed composition of a Cuban "country program" would be developed between the Cuban government and the aid donors, preferably coordinated through a consultative group chaired by the World Bank. Priority needs would be established and project proposals developed accordingly. The following figures, in contrast, represent a very approximate and illustrative summary of how the assistance, again keyed to the $800 million maximum level of aid disbursements, could be structured.

Technical Assistance

Technical assistance, in the form of foreign expert advisers, training programs, and analytic assessments, would focus on building a technical infrastructure for a market-oriented economy and for support to the political process of democratization. Technical infrastructure would include developing a fiscal program, creating financial institutions, establishing private property rights, privatizing state enterprises, and drafting the legal framework for foreign direct investment. Support for democratization would cover a wide range of activities, from preparation of free and open elections to the strengthening of an independent judiciary. Technical infrastructure support would come from multilateral development banks and bilateral donors. The United States has been most active and innovative in support programs for democratization, but in the case of Cuba, a lead U.S. role could best go forward in conjunction with the broader support and participation of the Organization of American States (OAS). Such technical assistance projects are generally provided on a grant basis, but by their nature they are management-intensive and therefore do not involve large sums of money. For the Cuba program, such technical assistance might be in the range of $50 million to $100 million.

Economic Infrastructure

Large long-term financing will be needed to restore and expand economic infrastructure to support the private-sector-driven economic recovery contained in the five-year projection. Transportation, telecommunications, and electric power supply are likely to be the largest sectors, and a number of specific priorities have been noted in this study: telecommunications, airport passenger facilities, and cruise ship docks for tourism and telecommunications, modern container ports, and air freight facilities for assembly industry. An assessment of the energy sector, including electric power needs, would be an early priority for the technical assistance category above. If, as apparently is the case, the partially constructed nuclear power plant at Iragua has unsafe technology and construction defects, an alternative energy strategy would need to be developed. Environmentally oriented projects would play a major role in priority funding for infrastructure. Havana harbor and urban waste disposal in general would likely be high on the agenda. Cleaning up pollution in the sugar and nickel sectors could become a joint financial undertaking for the public and private sectors. Overall, economic infrastructure projects, in contrast to technical assistance, are capital-intensive and need large amounts of financing. At the same time, infrastructure project financing should be in the form of long-term loans, concessionary in large part, rather than grants. In this context, the United States should create a development loan capability that does not now exist in the U.S. Agency for International Development.[2] The estimated level of infrastructure financing within the year-four $800 million maximum level is placed at $400 million to $500 million.

Social Sector Support

Social sector support generally concentrates on projects in the health, education, and small-scale agriculture sectors. The needs for Cuba, which already has broadly based health and educational systems, would have to be developed in the context of policies adopted by the transitional Cuban government. The resources of private voluntary organizations (PVOs), which play an active role in providing people-to-people assistance in many countries, would have to be adapted to the special circumstances in Cuba. For the education sector, there could be greater emphasis on more advanced vocational and professional training for a market-oriented economy rather than the usual priority aid programs place on elementary school education for the illiterate poor. One targeted objective that would best fit into the U.S. bilateral aid program would be the retraining of Cuban military personnel for the private civilian sector. The establishment in Cuba of extension schools of U.S. vocational training institutions and business schools should receive priority aid funding to convey a clear message to Cuban military personnel that they have more promising futures in a restructured Cuba. Funding for social sector support is placed at the $100 million to $150 million level.

Financial Intermediaries for the Private Sector

The experience of private sector-oriented economic reforms in former Soviet bloc economies and other developing countries is that the dynamic for growth comes largely from new small and medium-sized businesses in the service, industrial, and agricultural sectors. This will almost certainly be the case in a restructured Cuba as well. A crucial ingredient, however, is the creation of financial mechanisms to provide initial investment and working capital for such new businesses. These mechanisms do not develop quickly from the private sector alone because of the uncertain risks of new borrowers and the high administrative costs for loan processing. This will also be the case in Cuba, where such financial mechanisms will have to be created anew. The role of economic assistance would be to provide the start-up financing and some operational support for such financial mechanisms. The U.S. aid program has had long experience in Latin America in creating financial intermediaries for small and medium-sized businesses. More recent experience in Eastern Europe is also relevant. The estimated funding level for this vital element of economic restructuring is placed at $100 million to $150 million.

These are some admittedly rough orders of magnitude and content for a foreign assistance strategy for a restructured Cuba. The illustrative figures total $650 million to $950 million, with a midpoint of $800 million. In the five-year projection, the disbursement of economic assistance rises gradually from $100 million in year one to $300 million in year two and up to a maximum of $800 million in year four. This reflects the preparation time and relatively slow disbursement of project assistance, particularly with respect to economic infrastructure projects. Whether such a level of assistance will receive the support of the donor community will depend largely on how demonstrably effective the aid is in assisting Cuba's overall economic recovery. This demonstration capability is especially important in the United States, where public disenchantment with foreign economic aid is reaching an all-time low because of perceived ineffectiveness. In this context, an explicit strategy for assistance to Cuba, based on priority projects with clearly stated performance objectives, should be developed at the earliest possible stage in the transition process.

Notes

Chapter 1 — The New Caribbean Economic Order

1. Unless otherwise specified, the Caribbean regional economy is defined as North America, including Mexico, Central America, the Caribbean island economies except Cuba, and Venezuela and Colombia. Occasionally, for emphasis, the region is referred to as the North American/Caribbean region.

2. From a statement at the annual conference in Miami of the private-sector organization Caribbean/Central American Action, December 7, 1982.

3. In quantitative terms, the decline was from 1.5 million tons in 1980 to 843,000 tons in 1990. U.S. Department of Agriculture, Economic Research Service, Commodity Economics Division, *Foreign Agricultural Trade of the United States* (Washington, D.C.: U.S. Department of Agriculture, 1990) and U.S. Department of Agriculture, *U.S. Foreign Agriculture Trade Statistical Report* (Washington, D.C.: U.S. Department of Agriculture, 1980).

4. The volume of coffee exports increased moderately over the decade from 1.34 to 1.71 million metric tons, but this was offset by a fall in world prices. UN Food and Agriculture Organization (FAO), *Yearbook*, 1980 and 1990 (Rome).

5. From *Caribbean Tourism: Statistical Report*, 1990 ed., (Bridgetown, Barbados: Caribbean Tourism Organization), 47, 59. The dependence of the Dominican Republic on the U.S. market, listed in the 30 percent to 39 percent range (p. 59), does not include Dominicans resident in the United States, which are noted elsewhere (p. 47) as constituting 39.1 percent of total visitors. Thus the total share of Dominican visitors resident in the United States would be 69 percent to 78 percent.

6. See chapter 5, section on remittances, for the basis of this estimate.

Chapter 2 — A Quantum Economic Setback for Castro

1. The estimated 45 percent decline is based on studies by Andrew Zimbalist, a professor at Smith College, as reported in the *Washington Post*, December 26, 1992.

2. See Jorge F. Pérez-López, *The Economics of Cuban Sugar* (Pittsburgh: University of Pittsburgh Press, 1991), especially pp. 157, 199, 205, and 206; Nicolás Rivero, "Thoughts on the Cuban Sugar

Industry" (Paper presented at the Second Annual Meeting of the Association for the Study of the Cuban Economy, Miami, August 4, 1992), especially p. 3.

3. Central Intelligence Agency, *Cuba: Handbook of Trade Statistics*, Intelligence Research Paper, unclassified (Washington, D.C.: CIA, September 1992).

4. The 6.3 million ton export level was announced by Cubazucar, the state sugar company, on September 24, 1992. Subsequent market reports indicate that this level of shipments was probably not reached and that some of the 1993 crop will have to be used to fill 1992 export commitments.

5. The Brazilian import statistics were obtained from the Ministerio da Economia, Fazenda e Planejamento, Departmento de Comercio Exterior. The report on reliability of the vaccine is from *Pharmaceutical Business News*, May 15, 1992.

6. For example, from Donna Rich and Michael Kaplowitz, *New Opportunities for U.S.-Cuban Trade* (Washington, D.C.: Johns Hopkins University School of Advanced International Studies, 1992): "At the annual Cuban trade fair in November 1991, more than 60 joint ventures were discussed. Hundreds more joint ventures are in the process of negotiation. Cuban officials predict that the number of joint ventures will be in the thousands within the next several years" (p. 4). The prestigious Mexican newspaper *El Universal*, in a special section on Cuba at the time of the Castro visit to Spain, included this statement in its lead editorial: "In spite of prohibitions by the government in Washington, the Caribbean island [Cuba] received in 1991 between $400 and $500 million in foreign investment" (July 26, 1992). In his article "How to Invest in Free Cuba," published in *South Florida* (December 1992), John Rubino claimed, "In 1991, foreign companies poured about $500 million into beachfront hotels, golf courses, restaurants, oil wells and new telephone equipment, among other things" (p. 27).

7. Organization for Economic Cooperation and Development, *Development Co-operation* (Paris: OECD, 1991), 210 – 211.

8. *New York Times*, October 12, 1992, and *Miami Herald*, November 16, 1992. The $850 million for petroleum imports is from Carlos Lage, as reported in the *Miami Herald*, but it could be somewhat higher, based on world prices.

9. The pervasive scope of earlier Soviet support, informal as well as formal, is described in Andres Oppenheimer, *Castro's Final Hour* (New York: Simon & Schuster, 1992), chap. 7.

10. Oppenheimer, recounting the Ochoa affair, reveals in detail how foreign exchange accounts were handled in a decentralized and personal

manner, although tighter controls may now be in effect (ibid., chaps. 1 – 4).

Chapter 3 — The Castro Reform Program

1. For a detailed account, see Oppenheimer, *Castro's Final Hour*, chap. 14.

2. The Herrera statement was reported in *Cubainfo Newsletter*, October 2, 1992, p. 4.

3. Based on conversations with Cuban officials, Rich and Kaplowitz state, "A Canadian mining company, Sherritt Gordon, entered into a five-year $1.2 billion investment in the nickel industry" (*New Opportunities*, 8). There is no public confirmation of this contract from either side, and it appears that the company may be a substantial purchaser of Cuban nickel exports rather than a large new investor.

4. The official estimate of 500,000 visitors in 1992 is from Rich and Kaplowitz, *New Opportunities*, 21, based on an interview with Carlos Garcia, vice director of Cubanacán. The 13,000 estimate for commercially available rooms in 1992 and the target of 30,000 rooms by 1996 are from Eliberto Gracia, "Could Cuba Dominate Caribbean Tourism?" *Hotels* (October 1991), 41, and from subsequent private correspondence. The statement that hotel building has slowed in the face of low occupancy rates is based on various interviews by the author during the course of this study. Two foreign hotels that are planned but are reportedly on hold are the Spanish Cohiba and the second Jamaican hotel of the Super Clubs chain.

5. The $445 million figure is from Rich and Kaplowitz, *New Opportunities*, 22; it is suspect, for among other reasons, because it uses an exchange rate of one peso to the dollar, with the current black market rate reported as high as 40 pesos to the dollar. In *Business Tips on Cuba* (Havana: UN Development Program, October 1992), annual tourism revenue is reported as "about 250 million dollars" (p. 8). This article also cites the $500 package from Cancun, noting that Cuba "is by far the cheapest tourist destination in the Antilles."

6. Rich and Kaplowitz state that ITALCABLE will control 50 percent of a $41 million joint venture with the Cuban communications ministry (*New Opportunities*, 44), while *Business Week* (April 20, 1992) refers to ITALCABLE as having signed a $65 million joint venture (p. 46).

7. *Latin Finance*, no. 38 (June 1992): 28.

8. For example, Robert A. Pastor has called for Washington to end its hostility and lift the embargo, with a tacit understanding that the Cuban regime would later liberalize to democracy ("The Latin

American Option," *Foreign Policy*, no. 88 [Fall 1992]:119); Eliana
Cardoso and Ann Helwege recommend that the U.S. government "resist
the temptation to overthrow Castro now" and "remove travel restrictions and the trade embargo immediately" (*Cuba After Communism*
[Cambridge, Mass.: MIT Press, 1992], 113).

9. President Bush initially opposed the prohibition on U.S. sub-
sidiary trade with Cuba on grounds that it would cause problems of
extraterritoriality, but he supported other provisions of the act, such as
prohibiting ships that have visited Cuba during the prior six months
from entering U.S. ports.

10. The estimated increase in this context is lower than the projection in chapter 5 because, first, some visitors, especially Cuban
Americans, would be less likely to travel to Cuba while the Castro government was still in place and, second, state-controlled support services
would remain inadequate for some time.

Chapter 4 — Cuba Restructured: The Political Assumption

1. The need to distinguish between two stages of political transition
in projecting economic impact was first suggested to the author by
Felipe Pazos, currently senior adviser to the Central Bank of Venezuela
and formerly president of the National Bank of Cuba from 1949 to 1952
and in 1959.

2. The 60 percent to 70 percent figure is based on a conversation
with a well-informed U.S. official.

3. International Institute for Strategic Studies, *The Military
Balance 1991 – 1992* (London: Brassey's for IISS, 1991), 194 – 196.

4. See José R. Oro, *The Poisoning of Paradise: The
Environmental Crisis in Cuba* (Miami and Washington, D.C.:
Endowment for Cuban American Studies of the Cuban American
National Foundation, 1992).

Chapter 5 — The Cuba Restructure Plus Five Projection

1. See Jay Lewis, "Will Cruise Shipping Abandon the Rest of the
Caribbean for Cuba?" (Paper presented at the Caribbean Shipping
Association meeting in the Cayman Islands, May 25 – 26, 1992).

Chapter 6 — The Impact on Others in the Region

1. The Bahamas could be especially hard-hit if cruise ships that currently spend two out of three days in the Bahamas shift to stop at least
one day in Cuba.

Chapter 7 — The U.S. Policy Response

1. At a conference in Miami on December 5, 1992 under the auspices of Caribbean/Latin American Action, a distinguished panel of Cuba experts commented on the preliminary conclusion of this study. The commentators did not directly challenge the positive outcome projected for a comprehensive market-oriented restructuring of the Cuban economy, but the general view was that such a restructuring was unlikely to occur. For highlights of this conference, see the *Miami Herald,* December 4, 1992.

2. U.S. Congress, House, Committee on Foreign Affairs, H.R. 5323, *Cuban Democracy Act of 1992,* 102d cong., 2d sess., June 25, 1992, p. 1.

3. The Association for the Study of the Cuban Economy has held two meetings, in 1991 and 1992, at which a broad range of prepared papers were discussed. The meeting on August 13 –15, 1992 centered on issues related to economic transition in Cuba.

Appendix — An Economic Assistance Strategy for Cuba

1. A country case study of likely counterproductive effects on economic reform from large cash transfer assistance is contained in Ernest H. Preeg, *Neither Fish nor Fowl: U.S. Economic Aid to the Philippines for Noneconomic Objectives,* CSIS Significant Issues Series, vol. 13, no. 3 (Washington, D.C.: CSIS, 1991).

2. The proposal for a development loan facility, in the broader context of a restructured U.S. foreign assistance program, is contained in Ernest H. Preeg, "The Aid for Trade Debate," *The Washington Quarterly* 16, no. 1 (Winter 1993): 99 - 114.

CSIS BOOKS of Related Interest

Agenda '93: CSIS Policy Action Papers
Robert E. Hunter and Erik R. Peterson, project codirectors

November 1992   119 pp.   ____$10.00

In 51 papers, 38 CSIS scholars have addressed the most important issues the new administration must face during its early weeks and months in office. Each author was asked to pursue precise goals: to focus on what is most salient for the near term, to present the most plausible options, and to make concrete recommendations in a form useful to newly installed policymakers. Each policy action paper is limited to two pages and may be used individually or as part of a set.

CSIS Special Report

Agenda '93: CSIS Policy Action Papers (Supplement)
January 1993   22 pp.   ____$3.00

A supplement of four papers was published separately in January: Organizing for the Post-Cold War Era, An Agenda for Managing Relations with Russia, U.S. Relations with Vietnam, and Export Controls and Nonproliferation.

CSIS Special Report

CSISBOOKS 1800 K Street, N.W. Suite 400 Washington, D.C. 20006
Telephone (202) 775-3119 Fax (202) 775-3190

CSIS BOOKS of Related Interest

Conflict Resolution and Democratization in Panama:
Implications for U.S. Policy
Eva Loser, editor   1992   _____ $9.95

The manner in which Panamanian dictator Manuel Noriega was
removed from power has far-ranging implications for Panama's
political and economic renewal and for the role of outside powers in
that process. The distinguished authors examine the issues of conflict
resolution (both internal and bilateral), post-invasion democratization
efforts, and the lessons for U.S. policy in promoting democratic rule.

CSIS Significant Issues Series

Post-Communist Economic Revolutions: How Big a Bang?
Anders Åslund   1992   _____ $9.95

The author contends that it is time to take stock of the systemic
changes that have occurred in the East European economies since
the revolutions of 1989. Drawing from both the achievements and
failures in Russia, Poland, Hungary, and the former Czechoslovakia,
as well as in Yugoslavia, Bulgaria, Romania, and Albania, Åslund
focuses on similarities and available options and offers concrete
policy recommendations. He refers also to the different economic
transformations occurring in China and Vietnam.

CSIS Significant Issues Series

Order Form
Postage and handling   3.50 _____

All orders must be prepaid or charged.   **Total** _____

☐ Check (payable to CSIS)
☐ VISA ☐ MASTERCARD ☐ AMEX   Exp. date _____

Card No._____

Name on card_____

Signature_____

Send books to: _____

Send order to

CSISBOOKS 1800 K Street, N.W. Suite 400 Washington, D.C. 20006
Telephone (202) 775-3119 Fax (202) 775-3190